FROM
PRISON
TO PARADISE

A Story of Redemption and
Justice Not Served

FROM
PRISON
TO PARADISE

VANESSA ROLL

gatekeeper press™

Columbus, Ohio

From Prison to Paradise: The Story of Redemption Justice Was Not Served, A Life Sentence Was Dakota's Story

Published by Gatekeeper Press
2167 Stringtown Rd, Suite 109
Columbus, OH 43123-2989
www.GatekeeperPress.com

ISBN (paperback): 9781662911156

Contents

It's hard to turn the page when
you know someone won't be
in the next chapter, but
the story must go on.
—Thomas Wilder

Foreword

The words on the following pages are expressions from the deepest levels of my heart. I was blessed to be chosen to be Dakota's mom, especially to walk beside him through the darkest journey of both our lives.

Nothing written on these pages is based on scientific evidence, medical degrees or current psychological standards of practice, nor do I claim to be a counselor or theologian. However, I did mother a child addicted to heroin and complete my thesis on Adolescent Opiate Abuse, so I'm not blindly speaking on this subject. I'm writing from the standpoint of the experiences I've lived through and my deep love for my son, in hopes that someone may find the strength to continue their fight and believe in hope no matter what they're facing.

All I recall of June 28, 2019, is sitting alone in my driveway screaming at the top of my lungs, "This isn't the way the story was supposed to end!" But perhaps it was? The story ended with the most beautiful portrait of God's grace and mercy, and the redemption of Dakota's humility, strength, and loyalty. It's my greatest honor to love him, share his story, and be called "Dakota's mom."

Dakota used to recite a quote by Oscar Wilde: "The only difference between a saint and the sinner is that every saint has a past, and every sinner has a future." This story isn't meant to focus on Dakota's struggle with drug addiction, or the things he did to satisfy what he called "the monster within." There was plenty of media attention over all the things he did wrong. The victims have all had their chance to tell their story, and now I want to share mine. This is a beautiful story of God's redemption, mercy and grace.

It's a story told through the eyes of a mother who has had to walk a dark journey of heroin addiction, crime, an unjust judicial system, shame, and ultimately my son's death. This is my story. I have since learned the greatest sacrifice a mother can make is to offer her shattered heart to save her child's soul. There isn't a minute, hour or day that my heart doesn't feel the ache of this loss. I've encountered so many people with similar stories of burying a child. Yet somehow, I still feel lost. I still don't feel like I belong in the membership of grieving mothers. It's certainly something I would've never signed up for.

My prayer as you are reading this is that you may realize the great responsibility a parent has in raising a child God entrusted in your care. Furthermore, I pray that you fight for your family through everything life throws at you and never give up! My fight happened to begin with heroin, crime, and eventually, a life prison sentence. Your fight for your family might be a terminal disease, eating disorder, disability, mental illness or something else.

Lastly, don't judge. Everyone on this side of Heaven will face some sort of tragedy. Our response to this will be as unique as the individual experiencing it. Don't judge someone based off what you see or don't see. Please don't judge Dakota or me. We have sat in the judgement seat almost daily for seven long years, and that has been enough for me for a lifetime.

This book is dedicated to my hero, my son, Dakota. His strength and courage inspire me every single day. Further, I could not have survived this without the love and support of my husband; he has been my rock. I am beyond thankful for my other son, Derick, and still never take being his mom for granted. His presence gives me the purpose to get out of bed in the mornings. Lastly, this is dedicated to the countless family and friends who have been there for me through this entire process, and were praying for me when I didn't have the strength to pray for myself.

Pain has a purpose. I have been told, "Tell your story; it will inspire others." That's what I intend to do for the rest of my life.

Vanessa

(This letter is a compilation of messages that Dakota sent to me over his last five years on Earth. I used these messages to recreate a final goodbye that I think he would have left.)

Mom,

What's up? Not much here just chilling and thinking. I hope Derick is doing ok. I wish I could say or do something to help. I haven't been there for him in so long that I'm helpless and I don't really have any room to advise him on anything he is doing better than I did. I just wish I could tell him that things that matter now won't in five years.

I know that now that I am gone you are going to have tons of questions, so I am going to try to answer those for you now as I sit in heaven and you are missing me on Earth.

First, let me begin with none of this is your fault. I have told you countless times that nothing you did caused my actions. I hate seeing you so distraught over choices I made. It's so hard to see you hurt over something I did knowing I can't fix it.

I know the countless prayers you prayed for me and this is not the way you thought it would end.

I appreciate you very much even though it not always seemed like it I loved you and I miss you. You are my best friend. You are everything to me. I don't know what I'd do if it wasn't for you. You were the best influence I could ask for. I know after the appeal got denied you lost a lot of hope. I understand that but I promised you that it was all going to work out and it has beyond our wildest imagination, even if it didn't go according to our plan.

My dream was to always help kids with low self-esteem and shy. Kids that lacked positive influences in their life especially for a boy, who lacked a man. Boys need a male influence in their teens to guide them. It has to be someone that is cool enough to make them want to be around them. There has to be a way to find the misfits before they find someone that will put them up under their wing that is not a positive influence on them. A lot of people turn to drugs because you do them and the anxiety of not fitting in goes away. You feel confidence. So instead of sending our youth to prison and hoping they rehabilitate, which in all reality most come out worse than before they went in. We can focus on prevention instead of rehabilitation. I was going to try to figure out a more detailed plan because I could have gotten behind something like that.

When you get everything taken from you in life, you learn to appreciate the small things and the relationships you do have. My life was hell in prison. I hated it. But when you make a conscious decision to commit a crime you need to be ready to take what comes with that.

As a result of my decisions I missed seven Thanksgivings (my favorite holiday); waking up to seven Christmas mornings, seven birthdays, and seven long years without my family. I traded life for a dark, loud, maximum-security prison cell.

I know firsthand what it felt like to have people betray you who once said they loved you like a brother. I gave so much thought and action to people and things that were either negative or irrelevant. It's crazy how you realize who is there for you that the friends that I expected to show me support have disappeared, but family has stood by my side through all of this. What can I say it has been a reality check on life that is for sure. You were the one person I could always count on. You taught me there are no conditions on love. One thing I learned is to never let anything bad change your course of action. Always strive to be better tomorrow than I was today. There was never any obstacle put in front of me that I couldn't overcome.

Keep ya head up like ya nose bleeding. Don't let em see how low your moral is right now because then they get to thinking they won and its over. I love you mother. We got an army of people. People love to see the underdog win and that's what we are going to do.

Believe me when I say I am happy for you and that all that matters is your happy.

I started going to church a month before I died. I felt out of place, but I kept going every Thursday. I really needed to figure myself out. I did like it more than I thought I would. I finally surrender and accepted Jesus into my heart. Thank you for always standing beside me. I am sorry for what I put you through. There comes a time when you must realize that death is a part of life and everyone gonna die eventually, some sooner than others. All you can do is remember them for the best. I am sorry, I just can't live like this for the rest of my life. I will be waiting for you in Heaven, meanwhile I will enjoy skittles, microwave pizza's and my favorite- YOO-HOOS.

As for you, live your best life. The life you want to live no matter what people think! You only have one life to live and just because some people say this is how life is supposed to be lived, who says society is always right? Gotta follow your heart and your gut instinct on everything and anything. Love always.

I love you,

Kota

The Addiction

On November 16, 1993, the most amazingly beautiful eight-pound dark-haired baby boy was born. I remember rocking him in a chair, staring at him in amazement, struck by all the innocence and preciousness wrapped up in one little chubby body. I was awestruck at the perfection God designed. I was more shocked and terrified that God trusted me, eighteen and still a girl myself, to care for one of His most prized creations.

I used to say that if every child was as easy to raise as Dakota, I would've had dozens. Straight from the hospital he slept nearly all night long. Rarely fussed, if only to eat or be changed. As a child, he loved to be read to, ride bikes, and play outside. His favorite meal with biscuits and gravy. His most beloved people in the world were his grandparents who helped raise him. His precious little face would light up when seeing his grandpa, and he could get away with anything.

One of our favorite family memories of Dakota was his inability to pronounce the "t" in truck, so that it sounded more like "fruck." Everyone was initially in shock, thinking he was saying a cuss word, then due to the hilarity of it everyone would try to get him to say it over and over.

He loved dogs and playing with his toys, and idolized his cousins. He enjoyed watching cartoons, playing video games, and riding his outdoor toys that Grandpa would always tinker with to get them to go faster. Dakota ran around with a screwdriver from the time he was able to walk, and always wanted to "fix things." His favorite color was blue, and his favorite childhood character was Big Bird.

I remember his first day of kindergarten. I was so anxious and sad that his first five years had seemed to fly by. I asked if he was nervous and he bravely said, "No, Mom, I'll be fine." Little did I know we would have the same conversation a few more times throughout his life. His answer still remained, "I will be fine."

He learned to read well before the start of kindergarten, and shined in all forms of academics. His grades were always stellar. In sixth grade he desperately wanted a trick bike. I agreed that if he finished the year with exceptional grades, he could pick out whatever kind of bike he wanted. Everything he put his mind to, he not only finished but excelled. He chose a midnight blue bike and just about rode the wheels off, enjoying every minute of his hard work's success.

In adolescence, his kindness toward others was infectious. Dakota always wanted to be loved and accepted, and never wanted to upset anyone. The most effective form of punishment was for me to just say, "Kota, I'm disappointed in you."

He was quiet and never demanded to be the center of attention. He always made friends easily, because he wanted to be liked in any circle he was in. All his high school friends tell the same story of how Dakota was always checking on them if they were going through some sort of struggle or heartbreak. He was always breathing belief into everyone around him.

His high school principal wrote in his letter of recommendation, "This young man is very driven and his work ethic has improved as he has gotten older. I can see him being a great success in the future and being able to support not only himself, but also a family. I see nothing but good things ahead for him."

Every parent watches their child grow and has the greatest dreams for a bright future, filled with peace, love, and success. I often find myself asking, how did everything change in what seemed overnight?

June 27, 2019, was a usual Thursday, with me doing the same routine as I have every Thursday before, except this Thursday would be the day that changed my life forever. Stepping out of the shower at 7:47:00 a.m., the phone rang with "Pendleton Prison" on the caller ID. Naturally, I knew something was wrong for them to be calling me, but never in a million years would I have ever expected to hear the words, "Mrs. Roll, there's been an accident."

My heart sunk. I calmly asked, "What kind of accident?" thinking he'd been involved in a stabbing or a terrible fight. Prison *is* a dangerous place.

The gentleman just sat quietly for what seemed like an eternity. Then I knew something was seriously wrong. I started to scream, "Is my son all right?"

Silence.

I screamed louder. "Is he okay?"

Silence.

Frantic, I screamed at the top of my lungs and started to cry. "Are you telling me my son is dead?"

"I'm sorry."

My head was swimming. My world had just crumbled, and at that moment time stopped. I just stood in my bathroom with only a towel wrapped around me, sobbing and screaming, "This was supposed to be the safest place for him. How the hell did this happen? My God! My God! My God!" I then asked, "When, how, why?"

He said, "Last night at approximately 6:30 p.m. he was found unresponsive in his cell." Just like that, with one sentence my world stopped turning, I stopped breathing, and life as I knew it had been changed forever.

To understand the majesty of this story, I must begin ten years ago at the beginning. But before I start, it's very important to me to preface that this is *my* story of the events that have taken place. There are many people who have been hurt through the course of the last several years, and this writing is in no way an effort to downplay the effects that Dakota's heroin-induced actions had on the lives of a few families, including mine. Out of respect, I will do my best to not identify anyone specifically throughout my retelling.

The story begins on Thursday, September 8, 2011, at approximately 7 p.m. Dakota was beginning his senior year, and his little brother Derick was in middle school. I, as usual, arrived home from a late workday. I began my usual home duties of supper, laundry, and homework. That evening, Dakota sat at our kitchen counter and was browsing the internet for new rims for his Mustang. I glanced over my shoulder at one point and noticed Dakota slumped over, asleep...or so I thought. I woke him and told him to get ready for bed, to rest for school the next morning. His demeanor was not his usual sort; he was very hateful and aggressive, two words no one would've ever used to describe Dakota.

We used to always laugh that Derick's job in the family was to be my spy. He knew if I turned him loose, he was to sneak into Kota's room and find anything he could. Usually it was just a pile of dirty dishes that had been in his room so long, there was enough mold to make our own penicillin. That night while Dakota was in the shower, I turned Derick loose like a bloodhound. Go search! Within fifteen minutes, he returned empty-handed. Nothing!

My mother's instinct knew something wasn't right. A determined mother can do better research than the FBI. I went on the hunt. I pulled out the tray for his computer keyboard, as the first place I was going to was his internet history. Much to my surprise there were three syringes.

Time stood still, and I froze. I didn't know what to do, knowing my son wasn't diabetic and had no legitimate reason to possess syringes. I did what any mother would do, and called his dad. His dad's response was, "Calm down, you're overreacting." Overreacting? How could I not overreact? Something was wrong with my son. I knew what I had to do! I'm a Registered Nurse with a Master's degree. I save lives for a living. I could, and would, save my son. But how?

I lay in bed that night, not fully understanding the violent storm I was heading into. Dakota was a normal teenager and had done things that I didn't approve of, but those things always seemed to be short-lived. I really thought this was an experimental "phase;" I could express my disappointment, he would stop, and we would go on. However, little did I know this wasn't a phase. This was the beginning of walking through hell on earth.

I sent Dakota to school the next morning thinking everything would be okay. He knew he had disappointed and upset me, which he hated. I had faith in him that he would stop all this madness. I would come home from work that evening, we would stay home, I would ground him, and in a few days this nightmare phase he was in would be over.

I often think back to that night. I don't really know why I wasn't so hellbent on finding out the exact substance in those syringes. Shock, I suppose? I think I had sold myself on the idea that, whatever it was, Dakota was smart and determined enough that he wouldn't continue with it.

Upon returning from work that evening, I demanded to see his phone. He was very defiant and wouldn't hand it over.

Neither would he talk to me to help me figure out what in the world was happening to my son. So, I waited like a lion ready to devour. I knew something was on that phone that could help me figure out what was going on. Later that evening he went to shower, and I confiscated his phone. As I scrolled through the messages, I was astonished by the length of time this had been going on, the number of people involved (people I trusted at that), and the sheer number of message exchanges between drug dealers in Cincinnati and my son.

After hours of arguing, I sent Dakota to bed as well as myself. I lay there with emotions of shock, confusion, fear and shame. I cried myself to sleep. As I wept, I prayed for protection and guidance. I couldn't believe this was happening to my son. To utter the word "heroin" made me sick to my stomach. The next day I geared up for an intervention and detox, thinking to myself, *I got this!*

On Friday night, my well-planned detox was about to take place. Dakota wasn't feeling the best, displaying flu-like symptoms. I had been to the grocery and bought all his favorite foods. On the couch, I laid out fresh clean linens for him to lay comfortably on. I showered and posted up on the other couch, thinking that since he wasn't feeling the best, Mom will be here. We'll watch movies, relax and rest; by morning, this will be put to rest, and the nightmare will be over.

How more naïve could I have been? My little well-thought-out plan was nothing compared to the enemy I was fighting. At 10 p.m., the restlessness began. A few minutes later, he was sweating profusely yet freezing, all while vomiting into a bucket next to the couch. By 2 a.m., the withdrawal symptoms were something I had never experienced in my twenty years of nursing care. He was violently sick, begging to die, and so was I. Non-stop nausea, vomiting to dry heaves, leg twitching and diarrhea. This was Hell, but we were in it together. We both were crying. He lay on the couch while I was emptying buckets, keeping cold cloths on his head and rubbing his back, praying the entire time. I snapped a picture of his pitiful face and lifeless body on that couch to serve as a reminder that he would never want to touch drugs again!

By 4:30 a.m., I was searching every medicine cabinet in the house to make this nightmare stop. Nothing! Empty! No Imodium, Pepto or opiates. For a split second, I entertained going to Cincinnati at 4:30 a.m. to buy whatever drug he was using to relieve his misery. Seeing him so sick was horrifying! That will forever be one of the worst nights of my life. There was nothing I could do. This was beyond me, and I was powerless to the evil lurking in my living room that night. I was his mother and was supposed to protect him, yet I couldn't make this sickness stop. Instead we just buckled down, and I kept praying over him.

We survived those forty-eight hours, though, and I again naïvely thought we were in the clear. In my mind, I thought of myself as a nurse who had just saved her son. He had color back in his skin, the sweating had stopped, and so had the diarrhea and vomiting.

That Sunday, we sat on the bed and for the first time in months had a serious conversation. He kept crying and repeatedly saying, "Mom, you knew! You knew!"

I kept saying, "Knew what?"

He just kept repeating, "Mom, you knew!"

I swear I didn't know what he was talking about. Finally he blurted, "It's heroin, Mom, heroin!"

In total shock, I just kept staring at my beautiful son and his beautiful arms, asking him questions like, "Who taught you to find a vein?" and begging for answers. I'm a nurse and went through schooling to draw blood and insert needles. "Who taught you *how* to use?" I asked him. "Who taught you *how much* to use?"

He would never give me those answers; in fact, he took those to his grave, and I'm still haunted by those questions. I just couldn't believe my beautiful, smart, witty, charming son was injecting heroin. I couldn't believe my ears or the truths in my head. Neither could I imagine that after the weekend we had just survived, within a few days he would be using again.

Tough love. All I had ever been taught in life on how to deal with drug addiction or defiance was to practice tough love. So that was what I intended to do. Within five days of our horrific weekend, I had finished up an appointment when I received a call to come home quick; Dakota had been involved in an encounter with the police. Upon arriving home, I learned that Dakota had been stopped that evening with three other young men in a car.

During the traffic stop the officer noticed an aluminum can upside down in a cup holder with cotton and a brown substance, as well as four syringes and other drug paraphrenia. The officer also noticed fresh injection sites on Dakota and another boy. Dakota admitted to using and injecting himself with drugs. The other three adamantly denied using.

The problem was one of the kids was about to receive a scholarship to a prestigious college, another came from a very prominent family in the community, and the third faked an overdose to prevent an arrest and was taken to the emergency room.

My boys were always taught to accept responsibility for their actions. I failed to teach them that they do not accept responsibility for the actions of others. Four boys riding in a blue Mustang returning from a heroin buy in Cincinnati get pulled over, and four syringes are found. Dakota knew the other boys would face embarrassment and lose a scholarship, so he accepted blame for all four syringes. At that time all the boys were sent home with a "slap on the wrist" from the police, and strict punishment from me. Little did we know that more was ahead for him as a result of that night.

Upon arriving home and hearing the news, I wish I could say I handled it well; but instead I screamed, ranted and raved for what seemed like hours, while he sat at the table with his head hung in shame. After hours of useless verbal ramblings, I sent him to bed. I knew this monster was greater than me. I had hopes that Dakota would graduate high school and attend the college of his dreams or join the Marines, a shared dream both of us had had all his life. I feared telling anyone of our "dirty family secret," as the dream would all go away. However, at this point I knew professional rehab was my only option.

The next morning, humiliated and scared, I called his guidance counselor and disclosed the battle my family had been going through. I wanted reassurance that placing Dakota in an extensive drug rehabilitation would not prevent his graduating with his class. She assured me that it wouldn't. I called the rehabilitation center and reserved his bed. That night I drove him to Indianapolis and checked him in. Tough love.

Anger was an understatement. He was so shocked that I would do this to him. How could I? Like a typical drug addict, he tried every ounce of charm and lies to convince me to change my mind. I stood firm. After the substance abuse and mental health assessment, I signed the admission papers.

I had never felt like more of a failure as a mother than I did while sliding that pen across the line. I couldn't believe my once bright, shy boy with the most precious eyes you had ever seen was being admitted for substance abuse treatment. This was the exact thing I tried to shelter him from during all my years of mothering.

Upon leaving that night, he angrily slid a piece of paper for me to turn in to his teacher for his yearbook listing, due that week. He kept looking at me and saying, "I can't believe you're leaving me here." They escorted him out to the unit. I watched the secured doors shut and walked out to my car with tears streaming. Little did I know this would be the first of many goodbyes involving him going behind secured doors and I walking out alone, tears rolling.

Once in my car, I opened that little white piece of paper. "Who is your biggest inspiration and why?" it said. "Explain in detail." He had written, "My mom is probably my biggest inspiration she is very successful and had done it all on her own while our fathers were never around. My mom came from nothing and now makes close to half a million a year" — that part made me laugh because if only he knew — "although we don't get along and she may not know it, she inspires me."

Dakota spent a few weeks in that rehab center. I would make a weekly visit and see a glimmer of my Dakota returning. He was so excited to be learning and always wanted to share his new knowledge. He rarely spoke of heroin use with me, and I didn't have the courage or strength to bring it up. I just wanted my son back. I thought yet again that this rehab stay would be the end to this demon my family was fighting. After discharge, I picked him up and brought him home, thinking the problem was resolved. We were given our perfectly packaged discharge plan with a prescription for Trazadone, community resources, support network, triggers, Narcotics Anonymous meetings to attend, his signed safety plan and a dreaded diagnosis of Opiate Dependency. Everyone thinks rehab is the answer, and so did I.

Much to my surprise or disbelief, within a few days the school nurse was calling me to come get him. He was dope-sick! I was so angry, frustrated and exhausted. I could only respond with, "You need to deal with this right now. School is where his drugs are coming from. I'm at work and tired of dealing with this!" She tried, but he couldn't stay off the floor of the bathroom vomiting. I called a family friend to pick him up until I could arrive.

Once I got to him, all I could see was my sweet young boy lying lifeless on the bed. I loaded him in the car where we both sat in the back seat, his head in my lap. At that moment, I couldn't help but to think back a decade prior to such an innocent boy who once laid his head in my lap every time he was sick; except this time, he was causing it. I was fighting for my son's life and realized I was losing.

While in rehab those previous weeks, I had received multiple texts on Dakota's phone from drug dealers soliciting me to buy "dog food" and other code names for heroin. I thought I was doing the right thing by reaching out to local law enforcement for help, especially since these were adults trying to solicit and sell illegal drugs to my minor son. I was having meeting after meeting with the police, but they were only interested in details that might help them solve open burglary cases involving my son. I, on the other hand, wanted to fight the dealers contributing to this entire mess. On one occasion a detective told me, "Mama, there are no old heroin addicts. They all die."

In the end, no one helped me hold those men accountable for their actions. They continued to sell deadly drugs to middle-class kids from my little hometown in Ripley County. The police were only interested on holding Dakota accountable for his actions. Looking back, my naivete sickens me. They had no intention of helping me save my son. Their only interest was closing a case and assisting the prosecutor. Unfortunately it took me seven long years, my entire life savings, and my son's life to learn that.

Within a few days, the sheriff phoned me to tell me he had a warrant out for Dakota's arrest and was heading to school to execute it. I begged him to please not handcuff him in front of his friends. I knew Dakota would willingly comply. He promised he wouldn't embarrass him. Within a few hours, he was booked in Dearborn County Juvenile Detention Center on a felony charge — possession of a hypodermic needle — as well as other charges that came from that night out with his friends a few weeks prior.

I arrived at the detention center clearly not knowing what the coming days and weeks held for us. He was booked. Again I had to sign my name, this time releasing him to authorities. I was sent home alone, angry, and defeated. On the way home, I just kept thinking his entire future was over. There was no way he would graduate and go to college. Every dream I had for him died that night. That is when the grieving process officially started.

A plethora of court hearings followed, so many that dates and times seem like a tornado in my memory. However, the most significant was when the State of Indiana petitioned to revoke my parental rights. I didn't realize that was standard operating procedure for anyone in juvenile detention, but all I could think was that they were taking my child, just like when I was taken from my mother! It was unthinkable to me. Every defeating thought I was whispering to myself, they were saying out loud and adding a case number to it.

Then the anger set in. You see, I had been taken from my mother when I was eleven, and always strived to be sure my children never knew one minute of the trauma I endured as a child. Losing him was just inconceivable to me, even if it was just for a few days before he would be turning eighteen.

Juvenile hall was an experience for both of us. I visited every chance we got. We would sit on these cafeteria-style benches. I couldn't help but look around the room in shock at the young people who were "incarcerated." One little guy was the sweet age of seven. I still can't imagine what on earth he could've done to deserve to spend time behind bars, when he should have been playing with toys.

Dakota turned eighteen in juvenile detention. We still laugh at my ignorance when I called and asked if I could have pizza delivered for all the "inmates." They denied my request but did allow me to bring Little Debbie cakes. I think I showed up with twenty boxes of them.

In November 2011, Dakota was transferred to "big boy jail" on a felony charge of possession of a hypodermic needle. Due to being eighteen, he could no longer serve his sentence with minors. My heart sunk. Every imaginable horrific picture ran through my mind, from being gang-beaten to bullied or sexually assaulted.

None of that happened. Dakota was enrolled in a drug program and was excited to learn about cognitive behavioral therapy. He met amazing men who kept him on the straight path. I think he reminded them of themselves, just much younger. I would still visit every other week. Our visits consisted of thirty-minute conversations behind Plexiglas windows, using dirty telephones. I couldn't help but cry for 28 of our 30 minutes. I simply couldn't wrap my mind around the fact that this was where my son was. Seeing him in an orange jumpsuit, when just weeks prior he had been wearing his favorite jeans and blue shirt, always so polished, broke me to pieces. He would tell me all the time, "Mom, this is small things to a giant. If you're going to cry, don't come." I learned to hold back my tears until after the visit was over and just cry all the way home. Three months seemed like forever.

Tough love. It's such a controversial subject. I practiced it. What I've since learned is that if I had the last eight years to do over again, I would erase everything I ever did out of tough love. I've learned over the past eight years that unconditional love, just like Jesus shows for us, is the answer. That's what I ended up doing for Dakota. Unconditional love is vastly different than enabling. I never enabled him by giving him money to get high, or participating in any activity related to his addiction. Someone who has a desire to use drugs will obtain them one way or another, just like Dakota did.

I always told him he was loved, sober or high. I always tried to be there to support him in every form possible, whether it was writing to him or paying for phone calls and commissary. I prayed for him until my knees were worn out. According to him, I was his inspiration, but really he was mine. He was my son and we were in this together. I never wanted him to ever doubt for one second that his mother wouldn't be fighting for him, even if I was fighting him. God never gives up on us, and I didn't want to give up on him.

Drug Addict

Even typing this chapter title sends chills up my spine, angers me, and evokes the most disgusting feelings inside of me. Society portrays a drug addict as a junkie sitting in an alley, dressed in dirty clothes, uneducated, not worthy of the oxygen he inhales. That was not my son, and neither is that the reality of many of the precious people I've had the pleasure of meeting who have fought an addiction to drugs. I prefer to not label anyone as a "drug addict," as a matter of fact. I can't stand that phrase.

I've always read about sin in the Bible and attributed it to murder, adultery, not honoring the Sabbath, and other Ten Commandments behavior. But addiction can quickly turn into sin when one uses something — really anything — to fill that hole in your heart designed only for God to fill. The substance quickly becomes your false idol. Addiction makes a person sell their soul to the Devil. My son did.

The root of all addiction is pain. Their pain is real, and people medicate differently. Some of us go to the doctor for prescription medication like antidepressants or anti-anxiolytics. Some abuse alcohol or food. Some gamble. Some excessively spend money. Some, like my son, abuse substances like heroin. The result they are yearning for is to just make the pain stop. They used to feel something or not feel something.

I still often question what was causing Dakota so much pain. What was he not telling me? Why did he first try heroin? What did I miss? Looking back, I can see the sadness in his eyes that I never saw while living with him day in and day out. I pray the next time you're tempted to look down at or say something negative about a drug addict that Dakota's story will come to your mind. Instead of substances, every recovered addict I know has told me that they needed God, not drugs, to fill that spot in their heart.

However, for full disclosure I cannot say that has always been my view of "drug addicts." My opinion was first formed when I got my first taste of the devastation of drug abuse at the tender age of five. I was getting ready to get into a warm bath, reached into the cabinet to get a bath towel, and underneath there lay a syringe. My young mind had no idea of what was really involved around that little clear cylinder device with a sharp needle on the tip. All I knew at that innocent age was that something felt wrong and dirty.

In the following months that syringe would result in a police raid that involved the DEA dismantling every Barbie and baby doll I cherished, as agents looked for drugs in their little body cavities. I sat in horror that day, watching the police tackle my stepfather to the ground and scour every inch of our house, while demanding I sit on the couch and not move. Keep in mind, I was a five-year-old girl.

This syringe would cause my stepfather to abuse my mother and us on a frequent basis. I know all too well the anger of a dope-sick man, how quickly his anger can turn to rage, causing him to take it out on all of us around him in the form of domestic violence. I recall often coming home to my prized possessions being stolen to feed his addiction. This syringe would cost us multiple homes, money, possessions, security, and peace. By the time I was in sixth grade I had attended more schools than grades.

This syringe ultimately cost me my family. This was the most tremendous amount of pain and loss a young girl could withstand. At eleven years old I was ripped away from my mother and siblings, three sweet little faces who depended on me daily to be sure they were loved and cared for. Leaving them behind left a deep hole in my heart that I didn't know whether could ever be healed. It was the most unfair act that had ever been committed on me. I loved my siblings more than I loved myself.

His addiction caused me to spend years in a deep depression, close off my heart, and an inability to love others in fear that they would only be taken away. I never wanted to hurt like that again! Living through my stepfather's heroin addiction can only be explained as living in a war zone. Drug addiction isn't a solo activity. It drags every family member through its destruction and leaves lifelong lasting effects.

I grew up saying and thinking, "I HATE DRUG ADDICTS." What I have since learned is that often God will use the things you're most detestable toward to break your pride and teach you about mercy. He used Dakota's syringe to accomplish that with me.

I developed forgiveness for my stepfather, who I realized was also running from pain. As I have walked this journey, I've come to believe he felt genuine remorse for his actions and all the destruction it caused. Again, the demon was just stronger than him. Unlike Dakota, he didn't have many in his corner believing in and praying for him, and he paid dearly for it. My stepfather spent most of his adult life in and out of prison on drug-related charges, estranged from his children who loved him, eventually dying of liver disease in his sixties, terrified of taking opiates to relieve his pain. He died terrified of relapse. No one will ever convince me that anyone enjoys having their lives controlled by drugs. No one.

Fast forward almost two decades, and I was in it all over again. My entire childhood was being relived right before my eyes. I had tried so hard to change and break that cycle in my own little family. I couldn't believe this evil was rearing its ugly head yet again in my life, stirring up all those old painful familiar emotions of fear, hurt, anger and loss. This time, it was my son. My son who never met my stepfather, nor knew any of the events I had endured. My heart was breaking, shattered in a million pieces, yet so filled with an unconditional love for Dakota. I would never walk away from him. I would never stop loving him, injecting heroin or not.

The following pages are a snapshot into our lives for the few intermittent months Dakota was not incarcerated from seventeen to nineteen. To record each time or detail is too daunting and emotionally draining for me, and serves no real purpose.

* * *

I was again being lied to and stolen from. I hated it. I hated life. I hated what was happening to my family. I was powerless to control it. Night after night I laid in my bed with tears streaming down my face, begging "Why, God, why? Why my son? Why me?" I tried to do everything differently than what had been done to me. Raise my kids differently. Yet here I was again, in the throes of drug addiction. caused by my child, who I loved so dearly.

This wasn't supposed to happen to Dakota. He wasn't "that kind of kid." I remember, the day he was born Grandma Fraley said he was special. He always played by the rules and never wanted to disappoint me, yet his actions were defying everything I knew about him. It felt impossible and humiliated me to utter the words, "My son is a drug addict."

As I sat in that pew in the courtroom behind my eighteen-year-old son, in shackles and the familiar orange jumpsuit, it crushed me to hear him say the words "Your Honor, I am addicted to heroin." It was like this nasty diagnosis that sealed his fate. Remember, the police officer told me, "There are no old heroin addicts. They all die." Was I going to lose my son to heroin?

How on earth did this ever happen to us? Dakota would often explain to me that his addiction made him "a monster." It caused him to do things he would've never even considered without being under the influence. As time went on, I quickly learned that he was right, heroin made him do things I would've never imagined, stealing being one of them. I was in bed and had a prompting deep in my soul to look in my jewelry box. I jumped out of bed, opened my jewelry box to find every piece of precious jewelry I cherished was gone, including some irreplaceable items. The one piece of jewelry that never disappeared was a silver necklace with a high-heel charm with a pink stone he bought me.

I quickly I learned that Dakota would feed his need for heroin by selling gold jewelry, televisions or other items of value. When my house ran dry, he turned to committing daytime burglaries to satisfy a pricey addiction. He burglarized not just strangers but also my close family.

In May 2012, while he was incarcerated, I opened the mailbox one day. Inside sat a large envelope with the return address of South Ripley High School. Intrigued, I ripped it open. Much to my surprise, it was a high school diploma with my son's name on it. I thought it must be some mistake; Dakota went to jail in November of his senior year. I called the school and was informed it was not a mistake. Indeed, he had earned his diploma, and to my relief he graduated.

I asked how. I was told he had written the guidance counselor and asked to continue his studies. That was amazing enough; but more remarkably, I learned the guidance counselor had driven thirty minutes out of her way every Friday to deliver and pick up his schoolwork. He had never mentioned it, nor had she. In true Dakota fashion, he was determined to finish his dream and mine despite his obstacles. Her love, loyalty, and devotion were the beginning of the "village" that would soon envelop and guide us through this nightmare.

In a letter she wrote on his behalf she stated, "Dakota recognizes academics as important for his graduation and post-secondary goals. For this reason, Dakota remains committed to complete the rigor required for a Core 40 diploma... I respect Dakota for the initiative he continues to take. Dakota accepted what could have been a negative situation as a challenge to rise above and beyond."

Later that year, he was released from jail. Again I thought this horrific nightmare was behind us. He had just spent three months in a successful jail substance abuse program. He had learned so much about addiction, and gotten a taste of jail. I was certain he would get a job, and our life would go on in the direction it was supposed to be a year prior.

Yet in the form of true addiction, only a few weeks went by before relapse set in, and he was high on heroin again. I received a call reporting Dakota had been caught in Cincinnati stealing yet again. I responded with, "There's no way! I know for a fact that he went to an NA meeting and a movie!" Wow, was I naïve! Sure enough, he was back at sticking those dirty needles in his arm, satisfying the monster living inside of him.

The hours, days, and few weeks we had are such a blur. The nightmare was happening all over again. This time I had learned that neither a few weeks in rehab nor three months in jail were working for us. The police weren't going to help us, and my love wasn't strong enough to overpower addiction. I was still early in my journey of learning about addiction and thought, "*If* he loved me, he would just stop all of this." Instead, my home had turned into a war zone once again.

This short sobriety period ended with the police surrounding my suburban house, shining lights in every window, in the middle of the night. As I made my way down the hall to see what on earth was happening, there lay Dakota in the stairwell. He was so messed up on drugs and all he could say was, "Mom, I'm so sorry. I messed up big time." I opened the leaded glass front door. There stood three police officers questioning me on his whereabouts. My head was swimming. Do I lie? Do I give him away? Instead, knowing I was in a horrible situation, he pushed me out of the way and surrendered himself on my front porch. I watched in horror as they again handcuffed him, and off to jail he went. The cloud of darkness and evil is unexplainable unless you've lived it. Here we go, incarcerated for the second time for probation violation.

In fall 2012, just released again, he was traveling down the highway one day and blowing black smoke from his diesel truck. That was justification in the officer's mind to pull Dakota over, and so he did. The officer was certain Dakota was involved in a string of burglaries, and wanted to see if evidence could be found in his truck.

He opened the truck door without permission and saw a syringe, and Dakota was rearrested for probation violation. Years later, the actions of the officer were ruled by another judge to be a violation of Dakota's constitutional rights, and that anything found during that traffic stop, including DNA, was supposed to be inadmissible in court. But none of that mattered and no one cared. It didn't even seem worth the paper it was written on.

My God, how many freaking times is this going to happen? When will he ever learn? Does he even want to be clean? Does he enjoy heroin that much that he is willing to risk rearrest? I was getting so aggravated with all of this. His choices were consuming so much of my life and time. I still had another son who needed me, as well as a career to maintain. Dakota's actions were draining every ounce of life I had.

Failure to follow the terms of probation, relapse, all led to his first sentence at an actual state penitentiary, instead of the less intense county jails he had served in before. The judge sentenced him to another eighteen months, but this time he was being sent to a minimum-security prison. It would be our first experience with razor wire and prison bars. I would load up every other weekend to go visit Dakota. This was the beginning of many years of prison picnics consisting of Yoohoos, frozen pizza or burgers, and candy bars.

He was released in the spring of 2014. I wish I could say things miraculously changed and he had learned his lesson. Wrong. Nothing changed but me.

During the following months, I remembered a promise God had made to me a year before all this madness began. One Sunday in March 2010, I dragged Dakota to church. He was sitting next to me on his phone, paying no attention to the words being spoken. That service was one I'll remember for the rest of my life, and it provided me the hope I needed to survive a seven-year walk through Hell.

Our pastor was doing his usual announcements and opening when he abruptly stopped and said he had a serious message to deliver. He said that between services he felt God placing a message in his heart, and he was wrestling with sharing it. Am I so thankful he did! He shared that someone there that day was involved with something so serious that if they didn't change their ways it would kill them. At that time, I had no idea what the next few years would hold for us; but in my soul, I knew that message was about Dakota. I also felt an unexplainable promise deep in my soul that if I trusted God, not myself, God would protect Dakota and nothing bad would happen to him. This was more a test of my faith versus Dakota's actions, so I believed in that promise!

Within a few days, I was reading my Bible[1] and stumbled upon Luke 1:45: "Blessed is she who has believed that the Lord would fulfill what he has spoken to her!" That verse has become the foundation for helping me stand through the darkest times of our story. This verse became my life verse.

With any drug addiction, crime seems to inherently also be part of the story. Dakota was again stealing to purchase heroin, and police were hot on his trail. By now, I'm sure you're wondering why in the world I even cared. He was just another junkie and a thief. Perhaps to you, but to me he was my son. I shared my body once with this child, shared 18 years of his life, watched him play and grow up, only to be a heroin addict instead of a gentleman. To me, it was no different than if he had cancer; he was sick, and I would fight for him until I inhaled my last breath. More importantly, I never forgot the promise in Luke 1:45.

While he was serving time at a prison in Branchville, I received a phone call during church one Sunday. Dakota had been beaten badly by six men. All my mind could conceive was what he looked like on the cold concrete floor, surrounded by men who punched and kicked him mercilessly. Dakota was loyal to a fault. Where were his friends? Did they stay in their bunks while six men pounded him? What did Dakota do that invoked such anger that it took six to "pay him back" or "teach him a lesson?"

---

[1] All Bible quotes in this book are from *The Message: The Bible in Contemporary Language*, by Eugene H. Peterson.

Dakota had never been a fighter. He was taught "prison etiquette" during his stays in jail, so I knew he knew better than to smart off, be disrespectful, or owe anyone anything. To this day I still don't know, will never know, nor have any desire to know. Secretly, I was a little upset with God. I whispered, "Do You not remember Your promise?" I recited Luke 1:45 and couldn't believe this was happening.

Despite multiple bruises, a swollen face and busted ribs, he was alive for another day! I wish I could say my anger has been completely replaced with forgiveness, but I can promise I'm slowly forgiving by walking in the footsteps of those who have mercifully forgiven Dakota, a precious few of his victims.

We spent over a year and half at Branchville. I say 'we' because my husband always says, "Vanessa, you did the time with him," and he is so right. Addiction stole everything from me and my family. It stole my son, my peace, and my younger son's childhood. This was a rollercoaster I was ready to get off of.

In January 2014, Dakota was once again released. This time I was living two states away. I would be lying if I said this time I had hope that anything would be any different. Despite that, I still clung to the promise I believed God whispered in my soul in March 2010. Dakota did well for several months following his release. He gained employment, stayed sober, and tried to make the best of his life, yet he was still running with the crowd that always led him into trouble.

His pride was severely tarnished with the label of convicted felon. Job opportunities were limited due to having to check that box on the application. I would tell him over and over, "As long as you get up every morning and put in your forty hours, I'll send you money to get by when your check runs out." Every Monday morning until the middle of April, I would receive a call that he was broke and needed money. I never hesitated because I knew he was trying, working an honest job, and staying clean.

Then the Monday calls stopped and I received a different call, that he had relapsed and wanted to go on medication-assisted therapy. I said that if he found the physician, set up the appointment, and promised to work the program, I had no problems investing in his treatment. He did and made his first appointment. I was astonished when I called the clinic to pay over the phone, and they couldn't understand why I didn't just give Dakota the money to bring to the appointment himself. I couldn't imagine sending $400 a month to a kid with a known heroin problem. That would be enabling in the truest fashion. So for the first month, I paid the money, and he went to dry out for the first 48 hours.

With medication-assisted treatment, any opiates in the system can cause serious complications, including death. My friend was staying with Dakota during another drying-out process. At times it was too much for her to watch. She would call me and I would walk her through it, always offering to come there if he needed me. A few days passed and she thought he was in the clear. He had started his treatment. The problem was, Dakota was only using half his prescribed dose, sharing the other half with his girlfriend to help her get clean too. It didn't work.

Two weeks later, my sister brought Dakota out to visit me in Iowa so I could see him. On the way, she called and told me to brace myself. His drug use was at an all-time high. She was so worried for me to see him in such a state. She was right; as soon as I laid my eyes on him, I knew he had relapsed again. His sore-covered skin, pinpoint pupils and gauntness told the story he didn't need to. We spent a weekend together and I knew it might be my last with him. I chose to embrace love over my disappointment.

That Sunday, I had a decision to make: send him back home to prevent violating parole, or make him stay with me to protect him from himself. I chose to abide by the law. We snapped lots of pictures, hugged and said our goodbyes. That decision I regret and will take to my grave for the rest of my life.

The worst was still waiting to rear its ugly head.

On May 21, 2014, only five months after Dakota's release (much of it he spent sober), I received a phone call. "Mom, I love you, but they're shooting at me." Click! Silence!

I was still screaming into the phone, "What do you mean? Who? What's going on?" I sat in my car ten hours away, in total shock. I keep screaming while banging my fist on the steering wheel, "God, you lied! You promised me if I trusted You, You would take care of him! Luke 1:45, Luke 1:45!

Someone's shooting at him! He relapsed again! This is not at all what I trusted You for!"

Soon after my phone started ringing, and text after text started coming in. Dakota had made the news. The high-speed chase was the hot headline of the day. I couldn't even breathe, much less process what was swirling around me. Yet I was still sitting, waiting and praying. Was Dakota even still alive? Did they kill him? Who was shooting at him? Why?

The shooter was an undercover state police officer, I soon learned. To summarize a lengthy story, Dakota and an accomplice were followed by undercover police, as part of a sting to catch them in the act of committing a daytime burglary. After the crime was committed, Dakota and the accomplice proceeded to get back in Dakota's Dodge Ram with Cummins diesel engine and drive down a country road. According to Dakota, it looked as if they were being followed, so he sped up. Then he noticed two other older cars coming toward him, and he continued to speed up. At some point he lost control and they landed in a cornfield.

At this time, Dakota saw a few men dressed in street clothes coming toward the truck, still having no idea they were police. When one grabbed the driver's door, he attempted to drive away, and the guy in front of him fired several rounds that penetrated the headrest of his seat. Dakota thought they must be connected to the home they had just burglarized. The two somehow got out of the truck and began to run. I am not sure where they were going or what they were thinking. They were just trying to get out of there. Eventually the accomplice quit running and laid down in the field. Dakota looked back and saw him lying there. In his true loyal fashion, he went back and laid down next to him. It was time to stop running and surrender.

He was on the ground when he called me. He thought he was calling me to say his last goodbye. It still brings tears to my eyes thinking of the adrenaline that must have been coursing through his veins, the fear he had to feel. Yet he still dialed my number to say he loved me and goodbye before they shot and killed him. Once the dogs were released, however, they both knew it wasn't the homeowner but the police. They surrendered without a fight and were quickly arrested.

Meanwhile, back in Iowa, I had no idea of the details, only what the media was reporting. There had been a high-speed chase; a school in the vicinity had been placed on lockdown; and shots had been fired. I couldn't fathom how that huge diesel truck could even go that fast down a country road. How could Dakota be trying to outrun the police? I had watched him surrender himself to law enforcement before without a fight. Was he still alive? Do I get an airline ticket home? Everyone kept telling me to sit still. Those hours were the longest of my life. I simply couldn't believe what was going on. Again I prayed, and I believed.

Several hours later, my phone rang. When I answered and heard the words, "Mom, I'm okay. I'm so sorry. I am just glad to be alive. I love you," I was swimming in a sea of emotions, from relief to wanting to kill him with my bare hands! I couldn't believe he had done this. My goodness, they put a school on lockdown because of this! But my mom instinct kicked in. He was alive, and no one was injured, so I told him, "Whatever you do, DO NOT talk to the police." (We had repeatedly learned they're not on our side.) "Sit tight. I'm calling our attorney. Erase everything on your phone." (Why I blurted this, I still don't know. I guess it was just we had been burned by the police so many times before.)

Unfortunately, it took me several years to learn that the police are smooth talkers. They'll promise the moon and stars; but remember, they're only interested in closing a case and assisting in conviction rates. Still, he was alive! I found myself with raindrop tears pouring, screaming to God, "Where were You? You promised me! I've written Luke 1:45 in my journal a thousand times! Does this look like you protecting Dakota? I HATE HEROIN! I hate what it's turned my son into. I hate what he does to feed dope sickness!"

On the contrary, God *had* held true to His promise. Everyone who saw the truck was amazed at how those bullets missed Dakota's head. There was no explainable reason for him to be alive. He would call me and say, "Mom, I can't close my eyes without feeling the wind from those bullets brushing past my head." My God *had* delivered on that precious promise. Dakota *was* still alive. And more importantly, so was everyone else involved that dreadful day.

This was the beginning of the end for us. We both knew this wasn't good, and so did our attorney. Now it was time to sit and wait…wait for several long months!

The Trial

Soon the media was buzzing with the story of Dakota's high-speed chase. This lasted for several months. To read the articles and hear the stories felt as if they were talking about someone I didn't know. They painted my son out to be a vicious individual with premeditated plans to burglarize the city, and who *enjoyed* terrifying people. That was as far from the truth as could ever be.

He stated time and time again that he was dope sick. According to him and many others I've spoken with who have battled an opiate addiction, you will do *anything* to feed that hungry desire inside of you, just to feel normal for a bit. To be clear, not that anything he did was right, but no one was ever home or harmed during any of Dakota's actions. He never had any kind of weapon. His intent wasn't to hurt anyone; it was to get high.

People were so angry, and posted comments on social media like: "He better be glad he didn't break into my house, I would have shot him;" "He deserves to rot in prison;" and "What kind of mother would raise her son to be a drug addict that steals?" Reading these comments broke my heart.

This was my son they were talking about. My son with the most beautiful smile, almond-shaped brown eyes, and the sweetest heart I had ever known. I kept cycling between a plethora of emotions, from anger over Dakota's actions and fury toward hateful people to fear for the outcome. But two emotions seemed to overwhelm me most — guilt and shame. I kept remembering that day in the hospital, rocking my beautiful baby for the first time. God trusted me to lead, guide and nurture him through life; yet here we were, right in the depths of a disaster we knew didn't have a good ending. Like everyone said, I was the most to blame.

For months, we could do nothing but sit and wait on what punishment the court would want. I began researching long-term substance abuse programs in hopes that could be part of his sentence. I was willing to pay every penny for the program, as well as restitution to each victim. I found an amazing program in Hawaii and spoke to the director. Their success rate was the highest I had found, and the program was a minimum of three years. Dakota would have a chance at sobriety. Dearborn County would be free of the "threat" he caused to the public. When I posed the offer to our attorney, he laughed and said the only island they would be sending Dakota to is Alcatraz.

Finally, an offer came. The prosecutor was willing to reduce the charges to five counts of a class B felony, if Dakota would plead open at the mercy of the court (that is, without knowing in advance what the sentence would be). Each count carried a twenty-year sentence, and they could be ordered in two different ways: the court could order consecutive terms, meaning he would be sentenced for one hundred years total; or they could be concurrent, meaning he would serve a twenty-year sentence.

Dakota, like usual, told his attorney he would not decide "without talking to my mom." I, as usual, wanted to research what cases like Dakota's normally were sentenced in Dearborn County. Apparently, that wasn't the right thing for me to do. I emailed the prosecutor explaining I wanted to guide Dakota in the best way. I requested perhaps a history of cases tried in that county, like Dakota's, to see what their sentence was.

To say the least, he wasn't pleased, and due to what he called the "tone of your email" threatened to take any offer off the table. Looking back, there was no offer. He went on to state that Dakota had an extensive criminal history prior to his heroin addiction, and "it is clear your years of enabling your son's actions; allowing him to make excuses; and never hold him accountable for his actions has contributed to his criminal mindset. Due to this I am deeply concerned whether he will ever learn his lesson."

I was in total shock. Were we talking about the same person? *Extensive criminal history?* He was nineteen! *Years of enabling my son?* Was he there while I raised my son? I never enabled his drug addiction. *Not holding him accountable?* What in my actions did he base that on? *Allow Dakota to make excuses?* He ALWAYS accepted responsibility, and never blamed anyone for his drug problem or his actions. Who was on trial here, Dakota or me?

Based on this threatening email, I worried that Dakota would spend his life in prison if he didn't accept the prosecutor's offer, as per the email. I made a choice I will regret for the rest of my life. I allowed the fear of that man's words to persuade me to talk Dakota into accepting the offer.

Surely the court will have mercy, I thought. We're talking about stealing things, not hurting people. I watch the news, and I knew even most murderers serve less than forty years. God will once again prove faithful on His promise to me, and He would protect Dakota. In my mind, I was fully expecting a twenty- to forty-year sentence. Dakota would serve his time for his actions, right his wrongs, and be in his late thirties when he got out, with still a chance at life. I remember one morning in my prayer time, reading my Bible and thinking, "There's no way all these worst-case scenarios could happen to Dakota. He's *my* son. *I* have great faith in God. *I* have prayed and believed. I do all the 'things' that should make me and my family 'right' with God."

Then God whispered in my heart something that rocked my foundation: "*You* are no different than every mother whose son is spending life in prison." That sentence embedded a knowing deep in my soul that I didn't want to believe, and a humility in me that I had never felt before. I knew this outcome wasn't going to be what either of us desired. Despite Dakota's pleadings, I talked him into trusting our attorney, the judicial system and God, and just plead open. He wanted a trial, yet he trusted me.

In December 2015, I walked into that courtroom and picked my seat right behind where Dakota would be sitting. The environment was so staunch I could hear my breathing. I had never in my life felt such fear and anxiety. However, I also had such a sense of peace. This was about to be all over. I knew we weren't in for a slap on the wrist. I knew he was looking at approximately two decades in prison; but for us and the victims, it would be closure to this nightmare.

Dakota entered the room in an all too familiar jumpsuit, both feet and hands shackled, escorted by police. The quiet of the room took over, and the silence was deafening. The victims sat on the left side of the courtroom and our family on the right. There sat my son, ready to face his family and his victims, and relive every wrong deed he had ever committed. This time it was fear, remorse, and shame that would be coursing through his veins instead of heroin. Dakota knew his life hung in the balance. I will never forget the look on his face and the posture of his body that day. I knew he was heartbroken. The courage it took to face that day was unimaginable for me.

The proceedings began. I sat and listened to each victim tell a story of how Dakota's actions affected them. For the first time, there were faces behind the police reports I had read, precious faces who had lost belongings, but more importantly lost their sense of security. I saw their anger and heard their frustration.

However, one lady taught me a lesson in mercy that I will cherish forever. She had the stage, her time to tell all the horrible things he did to her, but then she paused. She went on to say that she hoped Dakota would get the help he needed to get off drugs and change his life. That woman, though I won't say her name, will live in the dearest parts of my heart. She gave us both the most beautiful gift — mercy and forgiveness.

We sat for hours as the attorneys made their case. Finally, Dakota spoke. With tears in his eyes, he expressed sincere remorse to those he knew he hurt and to me. He accepted responsibility for his actions and humbly laid his life at the feet of the judge.

That moment is when it dawned on me. One day we all will be sitting in that same seat as Dakota. We all have committed great sins, no matter our background, upbringing, or actions. God will be sitting in the judgement seat. Satan will be to the left with a file overflowing with every wrong deed you have ever done. Jesus will be on the right, defending you not by your actions but by His blood He shed for us. As for us, we will humbly lay ourselves down at the feet of God and plead for mercy. Will God grant us mercy and allow us into Heaven? Or hold us accountable with a guilty verdict to spend life in Hell?

A few short weeks later, we entered that courtroom once again, this time for sentencing. Dakota once again was escorted in, hands and feet shackled at the waist. There he sat, once again, at the table with two attorneys, a room full of people, and the judge. I took my seat right behind him, not proud of his actions but proud of his honor to accept the consequences for his conduct.

The judge began her speech and issued her verdict. Count I, twenty years; Count II, ten years; Count III, ten years; and it kept going. It was like being at an auction. I couldn't keep up with what was happening, yet this time it was my son's life we were talking about. Then I heard the word "consecutive."

My God, where are You? They just gave my son over sixty years in prison for stolen TVs and gold! Does this look like You're protecting him? I trusted You! I trusted the prosecutor! I trusted our attorney! I trusted the judge! But what ripped my heart to shreds was Dakota trusted me. I felt like I had just played Russian roulette with his life, all based on the email sent from the prosecutor.

Dakota stood shackled, strong and courageous, as they escorted him back to jail. I, on the other hand, was falling apart. I tried to stand but my legs wouldn't hold me. I was hysterical. My tears were rushing like a dam had been broken. I was struggling to breathe.

Once outside, I just couldn't believe what had just happened. The world was turning so fast around me and all I remember hearing was our attorney repeatedly saying, "I'm sorry, this isn't what I expected."

Reporters were in my face asking for my thoughts. Thoughts? I had none, only deep regret. My family stood surrounding me, trying to offer support, yet there was nothing to soothe my ache, not even heroin. Everyone was in utter shock over what had just occurred.

All the way home back to Iowa and the days following, I held my breath every time the phone rang. I just knew this sentence of six decades to a nineteen-year-old young man would cause anyone to lose hope and take their own life. I know it made me have thoughts from time to time. I kept waiting on a phone call that Dakota had committed suicide. On the contrary, the phone would ring and there would be my son on the other end. Just as I did his first day of kindergarten, I asked if he was nervous. He responded like usual, "No, Mom, I'll be fine." Dakota would often tell me, "They can't keep me forever…" "They won't bury me under these walls…" "I will never let them break me…" "Mom, this is just small things to a giant…" "Mom, I am so sorry for the pain I've caused you."

Small Things to a Giant

After the sentencing, we learned that Dakota would be sent to a maximum-security prison, Pendleton Correctional Facility. I had done all the research and read all the horror stories of things that have taken place there. My mind was swirling. I couldn't believe that a good, gracious, and merciful God would allow my son to end up in such a dark, vile, evil place.

There are two types of crimes, economic and psychological. Dakota's crimes were fueled by an economic desire, yet he was being housed next to people who had viciously harmed others for psychological satisfaction. I couldn't fathom how we went from the suburbs to a maximum-security prison, but there we were.

Months after that horrible sentencing date, I was finally allowed to see my son. I just wanted to hug him and tell him I was so sorry. My first visit, I pulled into the assigned visitor parking lot, stripped off all my jewelry, and rechecked my clothes to make sure I wouldn't be turned away for policy violation. I pulled a twenty from my purse for the vending machine, placed my purse in the trunk, and headed in.

When I looked up and saw the majesty of the brick building surrounded by a concrete wall topped with razor wire, my heart sunk to my feet. I had never seen a building so large, old, and terrifying in my life. Only then could I begin to imagine what must have been going through Dakota's mind when he first pulled up in the sheriff's van.

I walked through the first set of doors and took my place in line to check in. Immediately every ounce of breath was taken from me, and tears just started streaming down my face. The sheer intensity of our situation finally came crashing down on me. I looked at the emotionless expressions of everyone around me. They all appeared as zombies. There were two federal agents in line in front of me who turned to see why I was so hysterical and asked, "First time here?" Of course it was my first time; most don't have "visit a maximum-security prison" on their bucket list.

Once arriving at the counter, I handed over my ID, signed the roster, and wrote the offender's name, DOC #, my name, address, and finally, relationship. I wrote "mother" with the most pride I had ever signed a title in my life. They verified me in the system, handed back my ID, stamped my hand, and motioned for me to go wait with the others. I entered a stale, cold waiting room filled with lockers, stacks of old magazines, a dirty bathroom, and rows of plastic chairs. I looked around. We all appeared to be cattle waiting to be slaughtered. We just wanted an hour to be with our loved ones, and we were at the mercy of those with a badge behind the desk. One wrong look or word from us, and they had the power to take back that one-hour gift with no questions asked.

I found my locker, put in my car keys and turned the key, pulled that twenty out of my pocket, and filled my pockets with those little shiny silver quarters that would buy the world to those behind those bars. I took my seat and waited for what felt like an eternity. Finally, on the faint speaker I heard the word "Fraley." I knew it was time. I was finally getting ready to hug my son for the first time in almost a year. I proceeded to the security check-in with the large gray plastic tote; placed my belt, shoes, quarters, ID and locker key in it; then handed it over to the guard at the desk, who scanned all my items while I walked through the metal detector.

Next I was motioned to "walk the line," a long magnetic strip about one inch wide. In socked feet I walked that line, heel, toe, heel, toe. Ironically, it took me months to realize it wasn't a sobriety test, but yet another metal detector. Then I was motioned to a female guard who was holding a wand. Stand in front and spread your arms and legs, while they inspect every square inch of your body. Turn around and the wand continues, up, down, side to side. Then I was instructed to pull my ears forward and open my mouth. My thought was *what in the world*? I felt like with this kind of examination I should be handing them a health insurance card. Still, no matter what they asked, I willingly and humbly complied.

Once cleared, I was handed a small plastic container that held everything I could bring in. I went and stood next to the first set of bars, just like one sees on TV. The large metal doors opened and I was motioned in. The clank of the metal gate behind me rattled every nerve I had. My anxiety was skyrocketing, and tears started to well. Then I remembered all those times Dakota said, "Mom, if you're going to cry, don't come." For my boy, I mustered every ounce of self-control, and prayed for God to dry my eyes.

From behind a glass window I was motioned by the inside guards to put my stamped hand in a wooden box, to verify my stamp under a black light and show my ID. Expressionless, they looked at my hand and ID and motioned me to the second set of bars. I stood. They ensured no one was around to escape and finally opened the gate. I was finally in! I glanced around this dayroom filled with vending machines and small cube tables surrounded by chairs. I saw the guard desk and a cage where the inmates are brought in and out. My eyes scanned, searching for my son's dark hair, almond-shaped eyes, and smile that would light up a room.

Finally, I saw him. If I could run, I would have. My excitement was about to make me explode. He looked amazing sober. He stood in his khaki uniform with his DOC number stamped on the left chest. His brown prison-issued boots were polished and clean. His hair had a fresh fade. His smile beamed. Once I was able to hug his neck, I never wanted to let go. Finally, we were together. The nightmare of the unknown was over.

I knew our time was so limited, and like a true Fraley I just wanted to feed him. Any celebration in our family revolves around food. He ordered a Yoo-hoo, pizza, sour cream and cheddar chips, and a Nestle cookies and cream bar. As I stuck those quarters in the machine, I couldn't help but to think it was a meal a teenager would eat, not a hardened criminal convicted and sentenced to most of his adult life behind bars.

For the next hour, everything felt "normal." We laughed and talked about everything except prison. I just wanted to take his mind away from his surroundings for this brief time. I quickly learned that while sitting at the cube table, I was not allowed to touch anything of his, and neither was he allowed to get up, touch my stuff, or go to the vending machine. Trafficking was thought to be through this route. As rule-followers, we both complied. I wasn't hungry anyway; I just wanted to soak up every minute I had in this moment.

The emotionless guard walked over, handed Dakota back his yellow ID, and just like that our visit was over. Once the guard in the cage nodded, we got up and gave our final hug, and he walked away. Once he entered that cage, he just kept staring at me. I was fighting the pressure of a million tears from escaping my eyes, but *I would not cry* in front on him. The door opened, he went in for his strip search, and I cleaned up our area.

Once they were satisfied that I hadn't trafficked anything to him, the guard came out and nodded for me to leave. Back through the initial process: to the gate, show my stamp and ID, through the second set of gates, turn in the visitor badge and small container, to the locker to gather my key, out the front door. As soon as the sun hit my face I burst into tears. I was leaving him there. Guilt is the most overwhelming feeling I can express. I'm his mother. My entire assignment was to raise, love, and protect him. I was walking free to my car; he was being poked, prodded, and escorted back to a cage surrounded by hardened criminals. All because I trusted the lawyers and the judicial system, and Dakota trusted me.

We would spend month after month going through this same routine, sometimes with different annoyances, such as one time when my shorts were "showing my knees" so I had to run to the dollar store quickly and buy pants; or another time driving nine hours to visit, to find out underwire isn't allowed in a bra ("but this time we'll let it slide"). A T-shirt I wore that may have shown a shadow of my silhouette underneath; thank goodness I kept a wardrobe in my trunk. Or another nine-hour drive only to find that visits had been cancelled, over the death of an inmate who had refused to give up a cell phone and was rumored to have been beaten to death by guards. Each incident was cause to make me surrender my cherished one-hour visit to hug my son, both of us escaping from prison for one precious hour while drinking a Yoo-hoo.

Each visit, month after month, year after year, went on the same way. We would sit at that table with our prison picnic and talk about everything going on in the outside world. He would always start with, "Mom, how have you been?" I would always say, "Kota, I'm doing great!" even if it was a lie. Next, he always wanted to know what Derick, his younger brother, was doing. He followed Derick through high school, graduation, moving out, getting his own job, and his first serious girlfriend, through pictures and phone calls. He repeatedly told me one of his greatest regrets was not being there to help with Derick and to be a positive role model for him.

We would discuss his goals — never dreams, they were concrete goals! He requested that I mail him books on business and psychology. He planned out a business he and his brother would put together when he got out. He would ask a lot about people he knew in our family who had succeeded at building businesses, and take mental note of what they did.

We always got around to talking about his relationship with his girlfriend. Dakota fell head over heels madly in love at the sweet age of seventeen. At first I thought it was puppy love, but through the course of the eight years following, there was no doubt he loved her from the depths of his soul. They had a close relationship but were toxic for each other. They had dreamed of marriage and children. Despite their circumstances, he still clung to hope and love for her. "No matter what happens," he would say, "even if she's married when I get out, she'll choose me." Their relationship hasn't been one that most parents would be proud of. They battled drug addiction and made bad choices together. Yet through it all and till the end, his love remained for her, despite what I or anyone else thought.

He educated me on life on the inside of the razor wire. I used to laugh and joke that "when he got out" we would make a cookbook of all the crazy recipes he learned with ramen noodles. He learned how to give a haircut with a comb and a razor, make a hot plate with batteries, and a homemade air-conditioner with a fan and wet towel. He also learned how to make hooch, which caused him to lose privileges and spend some time "in the hole."

He learned more about respect and honor in prison than any man had ever taught him before. He learned to never owe anyone anything, and to never borrow without returning. He learned about the loyalty of friends, but the danger of trust. He saw how power can turn the kindest person dark. He witnessed the most evil side of humanity, one that most of us will never experience. He laid his head down every night knowing anything could happen at any time, yet he *always* remained positive and would never tell me everything that happened in there, and I was too selfish to ask. I couldn't bear the burden of knowing. I was already carrying enough guilt to feel like a million pounds.

I would lay in bed at night and wonder what he was doing, how was he feeling, if he was being hurt, if he was cold or hungry, or if anyone was extorting him. Prison is not a playground; it is *prison*, and people are there for a reason. I knew every day that many people were rejoicing, thinking Dakota got exactly what he deserved. I'm glad they experienced the resolution they needed, but I was miserable.

For me, I could never and still cannot rationalize how the judge, prosecutor, and defense attorney slept at night, knowing they had sentenced my son to over sixty years for theft, when he was serving alongside men who took innocent lives serving serving significantly less time than him. But despite my feelings, it was what it was. This was our new normal, and we would try and make the best of it.

After the initial sentencing, I hired yet another team of attorneys, this time to appeal his sentencing to the Indiana Court of Appeals. Every attorney, including our defense attorney, reassured me there was no way the appeals court would uphold that heinous sentence. These types of sentences are reserved for people who hurt others or have repeated patterns of this behavior. Every crime that Dakota was charged with had a dark cloud of heroin use covering it. Attorney after attorney assured me that the appeals court would, in fact, take into consideration Dakota's age and drug addiction.

The initial meeting was another rehashing of the same story, as quickly as I could without leaving out any details. Son gets hooked on heroin. Son commits crimes to feed heroin. Son gets pulled over. Son goes to prison. Court rules police violated his constitution rights. Son gets released, sober. Son relapses. Son commits more burglaries. Son involved in high-speed chase. Son sentenced to sixty-plus years for five counts.

I kept reiterating two factors that I felt were missed in his original case. First, nothing from the traffic stop was to be used against him, yet that stop caused a probation violation that landed him in prison for eighteen months. What happened to nothing being used? Secondly, the officer had such conflicting stories in his statement versus his testimony over the events during the high-speed chase, which was eventually used as a mitigating factor for such a lengthy sentence. No one was listening to me! I felt since Dakota was being held accountable for his actions, so should the police. I felt they were not.

The new attorney reassured me this was a cakewalk. I was assured this "discrepancy" in the detective's statement would be our saving grace. I was begging for a forty-year sentence, and promised we would go away quietly if we received it. He assured me that shouldn't be a problem.

Dakota had begun his own legal research, and felt certain his appeal would overturn the sentence he received in Dearborn County. He would repeatedly say to me, "Mom, don't let this get you down. Don't let them see you cry. This is small things to a giant."

More than a year later, during the summer of 2016, our appeal was filed. I don't ever remember feeling so anxious and excited, yet terrified. Now all we could do was wait, have faith, and pray, like what felt like a thousand times before.

Wait for mercy. Wait for someone to see that a young man who had committed crimes to feed an addiction had been severe and hurtful to others, but not nearly deserving of a sixty-four-year sentence. I prayed on my knees day after day, claiming and clinging to Luke 1:45. I just knew that God was about to do the impossible. We had been through so much already. I just knew God was about to bust open the heavens and grant me this prayer. Besides, He let me live through the biggest letdown in my faith walk I had ever experienced. I just knew He would show up big. We would shout from the rooftops. All of Dakota's supporters would be cheering. We would give Him all the glory!

The Appeal

On September 2, 2016, Labor Day weekend, the *New York Times* article "A Small Indiana County Sends More People to Prison Than San Francisco and Durham, N.C., Combined. Why?" by Josh Keller and Adam Pearce, shed light on the national stage that Dearborn County has profoundly high incarceration rates associated with the heroin epidemic, and that the prosecutor seemed proud of that.

We had been contacted months prior to the run to include Dakota's story; but due to our pending appeal, our attorneys felt it was best to not risk running Dakota's name or details, in that it might sway the judge's ruling in his appeal. The newspaper agreed, yet did feature his picture and the details of his sentence. They revealed if he had committed the same crime in Brooklyn, Cincinnati, or San Francisco, he would have received two to seven years, not sixty-four.

The prosecutor even stated he was proud that he incarcerates as many people as he does. The article also pointed out the intriguing fact that the prosecutor supervises the police force. To me, that sounded like a conflict of interest; but I'll never know for sure, so the people involved will have to live with their conscience if they were dishonest. What I have learned through this experience is the more powerful a person is, usually the more corruption follows. Through the experiences I have lived through and what I have researched in general, I will never be convinced this case does not hold more criminals than just Dakota.

In October 2016, I found myself sitting in a conference room trying to pay attention to my colleagues' conversations, but my mind was on the appeal. As I had done every morning before, I clicked on the link to the Indiana Court of Appeals. Finally, there it was! The verdict was up. I clicked on the link and waited patiently while the PDF downloaded. I quickly read through the words, sentences and paragraphs, certain they had rendered in our favor, expecting that God had answered my pleas.

On the contrary, they denied his appeal. My heart was again shredded into a thousand pieces. The walls were caving in on me. The exit was farther than I could reach before the tears started to fall.

I ran to the bathroom, locked the door, and slid down the wall. I simply couldn't believe we had lost. I couldn't believe God let me down again! I had believed everything I had been taught. Dream Big! Believe in the Impossible! Luke 1:45! God did none of that for me. My son lost his appeal. My faith was depleted. I couldn't begin to imagine how a loving God could allow us to lose not once but twice. My money was gone and so was my faith. In all honesty, I should not have been surprised. The same prosecutor who was after Dakota and I with a vengeance was promoted to chief deputy for the attorney general the same year we filed our appeal. For those who don't know, the attorney general's office is the defense in the appeal process. I will never be convinced there wasn't some political power play in the outcome of our appeal.

I called our attorney. Anger was the only emotion I was feeling, and all he could utter was, "I'm sorry. I didn't see this coming." *I'm sorry*? I was sick of hearing attorneys say "I'm sorry." I trusted them with the most important thing in the world to me, my son. Apologies weren't what I wanted.

That evening, the phone rang. It was my weekly call from Kota. As soon as I heard his voice, my heart sank and my voice cracked. He immediately knew something was wrong. He asked the usual "Mom, are you and Derick okay?" No, I was not okay! I was about to tell my son, who was so full of hope, who I had preached to for over a year to have faith in a God who will never let us down, that we lost.

Again, his reaction surprised me. He said, "Mom, this is small things to a giant. We'll get through this together. We'll figure out our next step. They can't keep me here forever."

Our next step? The only next step was the Indiana Supreme Court. We only had thirty days to file and funds were low. I would've given my last breath to save that kid. But something deep in my soul kept telling me to surrender and do *not* file. True faith begins where your ability ends. Surrender to God? A God who had let me down too numerous of times to count? Trust my son's life in God's hands when He has never proven to be faithful to that "stupid promise" of Luke 1:45? Trust a God who *I* didn't even trust anymore?

Yes, that's exactly what I did. I didn't appeal to the Supreme Court, I appealed to God, even though I was so angry with Him. I trusted He had a bigger plan than I could see. I still *chose* to believe in the promise of Luke 1:45, because I was still clinging to that 2010 promise for protection that God had given me. That was the hardest yet the most profound decision I've ever made. That was the toughest conversation I've ever had to have, telling Dakota we were done, that the fight was over, that I was tapping out of the legal system. Only God can do the impossible from here on out. Mom can't.

We spent the next three years doing the same thing month after month — prison visits, phone calls, and letters. Dakota found another attorney to review his case, to determine if there were any errors in the way his case was handled, and he continued his studies in the legal library. For me hope was gone, but he still believed.

Next Round of Cases

In 2017, we were served notice that the Ripley County prosecutor had decided to try and convict Dakota for those years-old cases that had been sitting on his desk. Back to court we went, despite being previously told that if he pled open in Dearborn County, all other cases would be dropped due to the severity of his sentence. Again, I felt betrayed by the attorney, prosecutor, and judicial system.

As I had done time and time before, I sat behind Dakota in that courtroom. This time, I didn't see the remorse in his stance that I saw in Dearborn County. I only saw exhaustion and frustration. I saw the face of defeat.

We listened again to a trail of victims with the same story — gold, TVs, etc. To be totally honest, after the past two years of what we'd both been through and what we as a family were facing, we were a little numb to another victim's testimony. It was the same old story. I didn't have as much sympathy this go-around for a stolen television or a jewelry box full of gold. This had now occurred years ago, and my son was already serving what felt like a life sentence.

I had lost a lot more than materialistic things which could be replaced with insurance money. I had lost my son. Every dream I had for him was gone. I would never see him married. I would never love grandchildren. Most heavily in my heart, he wouldn't be able attend my funeral should I die before he got out. My grieving process continued.

The night before his sentencing, he was spending the night at his old stomping grounds at Ripley County Jail with buddies who had never been the best influence on him, yet his loyalty overrode everything. When we arrived in court for his sentencing, we were met by his attorney who was beside himself, because on the eve of a sentencing Dakota had been caught in a jailhouse fight. Exhausted from the emotional rollercoaster I'd been on for six years, I just couldn't believe it. First of all, Dakota wasn't a fighter. The attorney was worried if the judge caught wind of this, our outcome in this case wouldn't be favorable. But to me, I didn't care what the judge thought any more.

We once again piled into the courtroom. To be honest, I sat there in body but not in spirit. To be quite honest, I was just feeling anger. Once again, my son entered the courtroom shackled and was taken to his seat. Once again, the judge ordered another long sentence on top of the sixty-four he was already serving. I remained emotionless. He sat slumped over with his head and shoulders down. We felt betrayed by the entire system. When would this ever end? God, what ever happened to Luke 1:45? My belief was drained.

During the months following this sentencing, Dakota's joyfulness disappeared. His guard was up. His tension was apparent like I had never seen. A cloud of depression enveloped him. On one of our visits I asked, "Dakota, what happened in the Ripley County Jail? With that fight?" He said, "Mom, that guy was a snitch. I knew he was about to testify against my buddy. That'll send him away for a long time, just like my friends did to me. Years of anger and frustration just spilled out. I can't stand a coward. He was giving up the life of another to save his own. You taught us to always accept responsibility for our actions and so should others. I saw those guys beating him up and my frustration was unleashed."

Dakota's loyalty has always been one of my most favorable yet destructive traits of his. He is loyal to a fault. His loyalty ultimately cost him his life.

The Welcome Home Party

On June 26th around 6:30 p.m., I was doing my usual evening clean-up after cooking supper. While vacuuming the floor, I was playing the radio when Ed Sheeran's song "Photograph" came on. It had played a thousand times prior, yet this time it immediately stopped me in my tracks and my mind went to Dakota:

Loving can hurt, loving can hurt sometimes
But it's the only thing that I know
When it gets hard, you know it can get hard sometimes
It is the only thing that makes us feel alive
We keep this love in a photograph
We made these memories for ourselves
Where our eyes are never closing
Hearts are never broken
And time's forever frozen still...
Hm, and it's the only thing we take with us when we die...
So, you can keep me inside the pocket of your ripped jeans
holding me closer 'til our eyes meet
You won't ever be alone, wait for me to come home.

Call me crazy, but I just felt my son so heavy in my heart that I couldn't shake it. I inhaled and exhaled several times, as I usually did to calm my anxiousness, and continued about my chores. There was no way to call him or drive down the road and check on him. I could only trust in Luke 1:45. I believed that God would stick to His promise to me that He would take care of my son, even in a dark cell in a maximum-security prison. That night I crawled into bed exhausted from the day. I nestled my head down on my fluffy pillow, covers snuggled over me, and fast asleep I fell, in peace.

The next morning the alarm went off at 6:00 a.m.,and I hit snooze for what felt like the millionth time. At 6:30 a.m., I finally rolled out of bed, inhaled a cup of coffee with sweet cream, and opened my Bible like I've done a hundred mornings before. Looking at the clock, it was quickly approaching 7:00 a.m. Time to get in a shower and get ready for work.

I started the shower, turned on the bathroom fan, and inhaled the steam filling our bathroom. As I jumped inside, the hot water streamed down my skin, and every sense I had seemed to awaken. I was officially ready to conquer the day! Stepping out to dry off, the bathmat fluffy and secure under my feet as I wrapped a fresh clean towel around me, all seemed so cozy, comfortable, and routine, until approximately 7:00 a.m. when the phone rang with Pendleton Prison on my caller ID.

Me: "Hello?"

Pendleton Prison: "Is this Mrs. Roll?"

Me: "Yes, it is."

Pendleton Prison: "You are listed as the emergency contact for Dakota Fraley."

Me: "Yes. That's my son. What's wrong?"

Pendleton Prison: "I'm sorry, but there's been an accident."

Me: "Okay. Where is he? What kind of accident?" It's prison. It's a dangerous place. This was bound to happen.

Pendleton Prison: "I'm sorry. There's been an accident."

Me: "An accident? What kind of an accident?" Long pause. *"What kind of accident? Are you trying to tell me my son is dead?"* At that point, I started screaming. All I remember is stumbling to my bedroom, holding my chest, and screaming at some guard on the other line, *"How could you let this happen? You were supposed to protect him!! This was supposed to be the safest place for him! How in the hell did this happen?"*

Pendleton Prison: "I'm sorry."

Me: "When did this happen?"

Pendleton Prison: "We found him unresponsive in his cell at around 6 or 6:30 p.m. last night."

Me: "Last night! You let me go to bed last night thinking everything was okay in my world while my son was dying? How the hell did no one think to call me last night?"

Pendleton Prison: "I'm sorry, I can't answer that. I'm sorry."

I think at that moment I entered a state of medical shock. I couldn't believe my ears or my thoughts. I couldn't get off the floor. I laid there and called my husband, Shaun. When he said hello it took every ounce of energy I could muster to utter the words, "He's gone." I kept screaming it over and over. It felt like if I kept screaming it through the phone enough, it would awaken me from a terrible nightmare I was having.

My husband said, "It's okay, baby, I'm on my way." Then my world went black for thirty or forty minutes. I just remember lying on the floor, thinking, *My God, how have You deserted me! I trusted You. I believed You and You let me down!*

I honestly don't remember the next hour. All I remember is my precious husband walking through the door and grabbing me, saying, "I'm sorry! I'm so sorry!"

My mind quickly went into mom mode. I needed to get my son home. In my total state of shock, I simply thought we would drive to Pendleton, pick up my boy, put him in our car, fasten the seat belt, and bring him home. On the contrary, my husband called Pendleton Prison and was informed it was time to pick out a funeral home.

My mind was swimming. I just picked a random funeral home in our hometown. My husband called and made all the arrangements to get my boy home. It took all I had to hold my head up in my trembling hands.

Our next call was to my stepmother, and she was en route. Next we had to tell our other son, Derick, who was living in

Iowa. My husband called Derick's boss, explained the tragedy, and said that we needed someone to be with Derick when we told him. His boss arranged it all, and even gave my husband the number of Derick's supervisor.

We dialed the number, and Derick answered. My husband said, "Son, I need you to come home. Your mom needs you."

Derick asked, "Why?"

My husband made sure his supervisor was there, then said, "Dakota has passed away."

Derick started immediately crying, repeatedly asking, "What are you saying?" He was so very upset. The tears started to fall, and he couldn't believe or process what my husband was saying. Derick was very emotional and didn't know what to do.

Shaun said, "Go home and pack your bags. We have it all arranged. We're bringing you home."

The entire rest of the day seems like such a blur in my memories. I can only explain it as an out-of-body experience. People started rushing to our home. Our phones were blowing up with calls and text messages. Social media activity was too much to keep up with. All I remember that day was sitting in a chair, unable to move, in total disbelief that this was how God chose to fulfill His promise to me.

Then I started remembering the day before, June 26, 2019, when the song "Photograph" had played on the radio. I had often told Dakota that song reminded me so much of him, because the lyrics say "wait for me until I get home" and "keep a picture of me in the pocket of your ripped jeans." I would've waited the rest of my life for him to come home. I know in the depths of my soul that hearing the song the night before had been prophetic. A mother's instinct is rarely wrong. It was Dakota's way of telling me goodbye.

I went to bed that night with tears streaming down my face. I was so afraid to close my eyes. I didn't want the day to end. I feared what tomorrow, the next day, the next week, the next month, and the years ahead held without Dakota. I simultaneously went into denial, telling myself that if I went to sleep, I would awake and this will have all been just a bad dream. At some point, I finally drifted off to sleep.

The next morning, I remember waking in a total state of anxiety. This wasn't a bad dream. This was our reality. He was gone. We had an appointment at 10:00 a.m. at the funeral home. This was a situation I was completely unprepared to handle, and we needed someone to walk us through every step of the process.

Arriving at the funeral home, my family was greeted by the warm staff who escorted us to a conference room. The questions began, as though I was filling out some sort of application — his full name, date of birth, social security number, place of residence, parents' full names, surviving family, etc. Coming up with the simplest of these answers was the most daunting task for my fog-filled mind. We discussed death certificates, newspaper printings, dates and times of service, who would perform the service, cemetery plot, and pallbearers.

All the details were coming at me so fast. No one thinks about these things for your child, especially without warning, and he was only twenty-five. I was struggling to focus and pay attention because I didn't want to miss a thing. I just knew in my heart that this was going to be my last opportunity to plan something for him. It would be a "welcome home party" (I refused to call it a funeral) and I wanted it spectacular, despite the fact that I wasn't in a party-planning state of mind.

Some family brought pictures and we passed them around while sitting there. One caught my eye and captivated my heart. It was taken at a much simpler time in our lives, before heroin, crime, prison, lost appeals, more prison time, and death. His eyes were so bright and calm. His smile so sincere and peaceful. That picture was *him*. I chose that picture for his program as well as his headstone. *That* was my Dakota. *That* was how I wanted him remembered.

Next, we had to pick out a poem for his funeral program. It almost irritated me to be handed three binders and told, "Look through these and choose one." I didn't have the patience for this. Thankfully, two pages in I read a poem featuring words that might as well have jumped off the page. It was as if the poet had written it just for me. That was it!

I'm Free

Don't grieve for me, for now I'm free.

I'm following the path God laid for me.

I took His hand when I heard him call.

I turned my back and left it all.

I could not stay another day,

To laugh, to love, to work or play.

Tasks left undone must stay that way.

I found that place at the close of the day.

If my parting has left a void

Then fill it with remembered joy.

A friendship shared, a laugh, a kiss,

Ah yes, these things I too will miss.

Be not burdened with times of sorrow.

I wish you the sunshine of tomorrow.

My life's been full, I've savored much.

Good friends, good times,

a loved one's touch.

Perhaps my time seemed all too brief.

Don't lengthen it now with undue grief.

Lift up your heart and share with me…

God wanted me now,

He set me free.

Then the funeral director said, "Vanessa, this is the last part, but this is the hardest. We won't stay in the room long. Tell me what you're looking for, I'll direct you to a few, and we can get out of there." I felt like I was about to buy a car, but instead I was picking out my son's casket. What was the most important detail to me was that it be black, gray or dark blue, with white lining. Cost at that point wasn't even an issue for us, as we wanted him to "go out in style."

The director was right. As soon as that door swung open and I saw all those caskets, the realness of where I was hit me like a tidal wave. As I was ushered in and shown options that fit my criteria, my tears were flowing like a river. I couldn't believe I was picking out my child's casket instead of his Mustang. I've always dreamed of picking out wedding tuxedos and grandbaby cribs, not a casket. Then, in the back of the room, there it was — the most beautiful casket, black with gray highlights, and the lining was the brightest, softest white I had ever seen. That's the one! Then *get me out of here* was racing through my mind.

Finally, I was told to get the funeral home his current picture and burial clothes. My heart sunk. It had been five years since Dakota had been home. I only had one shirt and one pair of jeans left of his. He made me give all his remaining clothes to his friend being released from jail with nothing. The jeans I had were the ones he wore from the high-speed chase, stained with blood but washed in God's mercy that saved his life. I wasn't about to part with those.

We went home and picked out an outfit Dakota would have approved of — buckle jeans and a blue button-up shirt with short sleeves that ensured his tattoos showed. He loved to dress nice and be "polished," as he would say. I was going to ensure at his final welcome home party that he would look stunning.

We had four days until the "party." During those days, our house was filled with visitors who just wanted to shower us with love. Everyone brought pictures, stories or memories. I don't know how I could've gotten through that weekend without each person who showed up for myself, Derick, and my husband.

By Monday evening the visitors had stopped coming, and my husband took Derick into the woods to clear their heads and find some peace. I felt like I just needed to be by myself, so they went on their way. I just sat in our driveway, finally starting to feel again. It was the first time I'd been alone since receiving that phone call four days prior. My chest felt like it was starting to cave, my anxiety was rising, and my anger was boiling.

I just kept screaming at the top of my lungs, full of anger at God, "This wasn't the way our story was supposed to end! Why? Was it not enough for You to let us live through a heroin addiction? I stayed faithful. We walked through jail terms. I stayed faithful. He went to prison. I stayed faithful. We were given an unreasonable sixty-four-year sentence. I stayed faithful. We lost our appeal. I stayed faithful. We went through another court hearing that netted an additional twenty-year sentence in prison. I stayed faithful. And for all that faith, you rewarded me by taking my son?" Everything I had ever believed about a loving God came crashing down around me in that instant. Luke 1:45 was a joke to me.

The next morning was the "welcome home party." Being that it was on a Tuesday morning, we didn't expect a huge turnout. Dakota had been gone from home for five years. Despite that, we had planned the music, balloons filled the room, there was a cooler of Yoo-hoos for toasting, and the most beautiful "Welcome Home" banner was hanging on the back of his "Mustang" (we refused to call it a casket). Dakota loved Mustangs and owned three. Nothing was more fitting than to call it that. Our only regrets of that day were not putting a 5.0 emblem on his casket, and not ensuring they give him a clean fade with a straight line. His hair was very important to him.

We arrived early and they let us in. I walked through those double doors. In front of that room was the most beautiful black "Mustang" with white interior. There laid my beautiful boy. My heart sunk. I just couldn't get to him fast enough. As soon as I stood by his side, I just couldn't stop patting his precious hands. This was unlike any visit we had ever had before. This goodbye was going to be the hardest for sure, because it would be our last. I wouldn't allow myself to even go there. As I had promised him time and time again, I would try to not cry for the next few hours. We were here to celebrate.

At 11:00 a.m., friends and family started trickling in. Once again, I took my place next to Dakota, with my husband and Derick. We were going to be strong for every person who would bless us with their time to come show respect and say goodbye to my beloved boy. At one point I looked up and the line was as far as my eye could see. This was amazing. On a Tuesday morning, this many people had been touched enough by Dakota to come visit us. Our gratitude can never be described in words.

One special visitor hugged my neck; his guidance counselor from school. I finally got the opportunity to tell her what I've told so many others about how her generosity and kindness ensured that my son received his high school diploma.

Friend after friend, family after family said their goodbyes, hugged us, and patiently took their seats. One of his friends said, "I just saw him on Monday, and he looked great!"

I said, "What do you mean you just saw him Monday?"

She said, "He was in Ripley County Court."

I smiled and hugged her. I thought she had her dates wrong, because I didn't know of a court hearing that past Monday, and he had never said anything. I would've been there. I was quickly on to the next friend's condolences, yet I tucked that comment away to process later.

Scott and Christy, our family friends, performed the most special service to honor Dakota and his life. They blessed me by playing "Photograph" in the middle of his service. I wanted one distinct message to be spoken about him, and that was redemption. I couldn't explain it at the time because I was still so angry at God, but I couldn't shake the word 'redemption.' Scott delivered beyond my expectations.

Once the service was over and everyone left the room, I made my way up to the casket for one last opportunity to be with him, just the two of us. Those few moments are some I will cherish forever. I knelt next to the casket, held his hand, told him I loved him and was so proud to be chosen to be his mom. I told him to wait for me, just like I waited for him. I can still feel the stillness of kneeling next to him yet the unbelief that this was finally our good-bye.

Everyone drove out to the cemetery. We had picked a beautiful spot next to a cornfield, a few rows behind his grandparents (two of his favorite people). The ceremony was beautiful. Scott prayed and Christy played "Amazing Grace," my favorite song. Someone brought a silver paint marker and we all signed farewell wishes on Dakota's mustang. Mine was "I am so proud to be your mom and I will love you forever."

The grand finale was a Yoo-hoo toast with a beautiful balloon release. It was the most peace I had felt since before June 26, 2019. As I watched those balloons go up and up, so slowly and softly, it was as if a part of my soul went with them.

Later that night, I placed on a shelf in my living room a beautiful battery-operated lantern my friend had brought to the funeral home. I texted her a picture and thanked her for such a thoughtful gift. The lantern was off. Exhausted from the day, I laid on my pillow with tears streaming and a shattered heart. I prayed that God would just please let me know that Dakota was in Heaven. At this time I still didn't know how he had died. I just needed to know that he was in Heaven. It was my last thing to believe in for Dakota. I prayed God wouldn't let me down again. Off to sleep I went.

The next day we were hustling around the house, which was filled with gifts, flowers, and funeralthings. We needed to get to the airport to pick up Derick's girlfriend, who was flying in to stay the weekend with us. I had passed that shelf in my living room several times that day, and the lantern was off. At around 1:00 p.m.,I noticed the lantern candle was on. My first thought was, *Oh, that's the sweetest. My husband turned it on.* When I asked him, he said that no, it hadn't been him. He suggested that maybe Derick did it, but when I asked Derick he also said no, admitting that he immediately had chills and goosebumps. When I read the words on the lantern, it dawned on me that God turned it on to answer my question of whether Dakota was in Heaven:

Perhaps they are not stars in the sky, but rather openings where our loved ones shine down to let us know they are happy.

From that moment on, I've never questioned where Dakota is, only how and why he got there.

The 5th Box

The funeral was over. Everyone went back to work, including me. I was trying so hard to just grieve "normally," whatever that meant. I was obsessed with finding out how Dakota died. Why didn't he say goodbye? Nothing made sense.

At his funeral there were things that just didn't feel or look right to me. For example, it appeared his nose bridge was bruised, and the right side of his neck was significantly swollen. All we were getting from the prison was to wait on the autopsy and that "he was a known drug addict." They suspected a drug overdose, except I had a real problem with that theory. I knew Dakota better than anyone. I had seen him every month for the last five years. If he had relapsed, I would've been the first to spot it. He didn't relapse, despite the pretty, neatly packaged explanation they were trying to sell me.

As a matter of fact, they were not very generous at all with sharing any information. So, I reached out to the EMS department that had arrived that evening and performed CPR. I spoke to the coroner and received their report. I attempted several times to speak with someone from the

Indiana State Police and Pendleton Prison to just provide me answers to my questions. They didn't feel obliged to assist me, so on to the Indiana Governor's Office I went. Again, that was a disappointment. It's all political jargon to get you to just go away.

According to the coroner's report, Dakota was last observed going into his cell, alone, at approximately 3:30 p.m. At approximately 5:30 p.m., Dakota was found collapsed in a locked cell, alone, by a fellow inmate mopping the hall. Furthermore, the report states that once the inmate saw Dakota slumped over, he began to throw water on him and alerted the guards. The guards arrived and placed him on a backboard, at one point allowing his head to fall off and sustain a laceration from hitting the floor. The guards were met by a nurse who wanted them to stop so she could assess. They refused and kept on going. Once in the infirmary, EMS arrived to find my baby dead on a table, handcuffed and shackled at the waist and ankles, in a white T-shirt and black prison-issue shorts.

For weeks I imagined every horrific, tragic event I could possibly think of that led to the death of my son. The words of a professional who saw Dakota's body kept ringing in my ears: "His neck was so swollen, it appeared he hung himself." I argued against that because there were no ligature marks, and he never left me a note.

Based on that professional opinion, the lack of cooperation, and the pending investigation of the prison incident Dakota had been involved in only a few weeks prior, my only plausible explanation was he had been choked to death by a guard. They were the only ones who would've had access to him between 3:30 p.m. and 5:30 p.m. No one at the prison, state police, or governor's office was interested in that theory, obviously. Day after day, night after night, I continued to go to bed haunted by this unsolved question.

Two weeks later the autopsy report came in. Positive for fentanyl overdose. That led to an entirely different set of questions. Did I miss something? Did he relapse? Where and how did he get fentanyl? Why weren't the guards checking him like they were supposed to, according to their policy? Did they have the autopsy report mixed up?

Nothing made sense. If anything, I was more confused. Dakota was always so careful to never buy heroin that could even possibly be laced with fentanyl. He was afraid of dying and terrified of fentanyl. Furthermore, reading through his entire prison record finally given to me, there was never any mention of recent drug use.

Another call I made was to his attorney who represented his last court case in Ripley County. I asked about the comment his friend made at the "welcome home party" about seeing him in court that Monday. I was certain she had her dates wrong or saw someone who resembled him. The attorney soberly replied, "I'm sorry to tell you this, but Dakota was in court Monday. I asked him, 'Where's your mom?' and he said, 'I don't want her to know about this. I don't want to bother her anymore or cause her any more stress.' I'm so sorry to have to tell you this."

I quickly learned that at that Monday hearing, they were sentencing him to possibly another twenty years for that jailhouse fight, for an approximate total sentence of 84 years. Dakota would be over a hundred years old before he could walk out of prison a free man for burglary and a jailhouse fight. The room was spinning. I couldn't believe what I was hearing. I couldn't believe Dakota didn't tell me. I could've at least had one more opportunity to see him and tell him I loved him. None of this still explained the fentanyl.

Two long months went by before we could drive to Pendleton and bring my son's belongings home. In a matter of fifteen minutes and seven boxes, Dakota's things were finally out of the confines of "the wall" and razor wire. We were so careful with those boxes. Once we arrived home, my husband cleared out a space and neatly placed every one of Dakota's treasured belongings in those cardboard boxes in its safe place. He told me, "Vanessa, just take your time."

To me it was the saddest yet most exhilarating moment, wrapped into one. I was so sad to open those boxes and see his sunglasses, toothbrush, comb, headphones, fan, and pictures. My goodness, he had tons of pictures. The next box was filled with hygiene products such as soap, deodorant, and toothpaste. At least I taught him how to be clean! Two boxes contained books. He loved to read and read a variety of authors. In those boxes, I found his Bible. I wish I had a dollar for how many Bibles I mailed him, so to find this one was so special, despite the fact that it looked like it had never been opened.

The fifth box contained what appeared to be important paperwork and lots of it. I knew this box would take a while. So up the stairs I went, toting this heavy box out to the barn where my husband was. I was so looking forward to going through this box page by page. Finding a seat, I planted the box down between my feet and started at the top. About halfway in I found a white piece of paper containing his commissary receipt for the month of May. I was so excited to see what all he ordered. Much to my surprise, the large writing on the back caught my eye. I flipped it over and there I couldn't believe what I was seeing. "DO NOT RESCUTATE. DO NOT."

My God! He died by suicide! That totally explained the fentanyl, but now the broken pieces of my heart were completely crushed into ash. He gave up! He promised he would never give up! He made me promise to never give up, to always "keep my nose up like ya nose is bleeding!"

I called my aunt. My first question was, "Why didn't he at least call me to say goodbye?"

She said, "Honey, he knew hearing your voice would take away any courage he had to do it."

I kept digging in the box. I finally found a letter he had written to me on Mother's Day and never mailed. The last paragraph said, "Mom, live your best life!" I was crushed! Being a mom and a wife *was* my best life, and now a part of it had been ripped from me. That was my final letter. I *knew* he would never leave me without a letter.

Finally, it all began to make some sort of sense. It was finally sinking in. It was over. Finished. The last chapter of the story was written. He let them win. He would die inside the wall, alone. He let them bury him under the walls of razor wire. I was so angry, but how could I blame him?

Prison Saved My Life

In Dakota's final statement to the court, he stood tall in his jail-issued jumpsuit and humbly said, "Prison saved my life." Since his death those words have haunted me over and over. When the prison guard called me to let me know Dakota had died, alone, in a prison cell, Dakota's words kept echoing in my ears. I kept screaming, "This was supposed to be the safest place for him. How could he have died?"

In all my visits with him, I watched month after month the brightness in his eyes fade to dark. I so many times wanted to ask what it was like in there; how he was feeling? I just never could bring myself to it. I knew I could not handle the truth. I also just would like to know who gave him that fatal dose of fentanyl. Did he say anything to them? Did they know they were assisting in suicide?

Since his passing, I have researched this place that was supposed to save his life. I have studied at the feet of those who have lived where he was. I have immersed myself into the dark world of the criminal justice system. Having never seen the inside of a prison cell, or felt the concrete bunks of the isolation wing, I am going to do my best to take you into the world most of us will never know.

Society has a fascination with the punishment of criminals. We often carry our pitchforks and torches, demanding that society "put them in a cage and throw away the key," even if the time does not fit the crime. I am all for justice. We knew and never hid the fact that Dakota committed crimes and that there were victims. All I ever asked for was a fair sentence. I also wanted it to be loudly known that Dakota's actions were fueled by a substance abuse addiction and that he wasn't some sadistic person who enjoyed breaking into people's houses. On the contrary, he was very ashamed. I can never imagine a time as a child where he might ask for a heroin-addicted criminal G.I. Joe action figure for Christmas or his birthday.

Prison is to serve four main purposes: retribution, incapacitation, deterrance, and rehabilitation. It is a place to isolate those who have broken societal standards and public policy. Dakota became addicted to heroin and thus broke a societal standard. He went on to commit burglary, violating public policy, which has consequences. For him it was sixty-seven years and possibly twenty more in a maximum-security prison.

From discussions with our attorneys I had learned that several factors come into play when determining the length of sentencing for burglary. Those include the type of property stolen, whether there were people home, whether he had a weapon, whether he under the influence of drugs, and his intent. As I have stated before, there were never people home, he never had a weapon, and his motivating factor was not vicious intent, yet rather to feed a horrible addiction. No one I have talked to can even fathom how the judge can justify the sentence she gave to Dakota.

I sometimes will allow my mind to take me to the place many have told me about. Prison is an emotionally cold, colorless place filled with people who are always on guard. You are to never trust anyone, borrow from anyone, or owe anyone anything. Your life will depend on it. People who are housed in maximum security prison have committed some of the most heinous crimes that exist, such as calculated murder, rape, gross molestation of children and sex trafficking. And then you have a twenty-year-old man who stole some televisions and gold.

Some of the dorms he was in consisted of a vast room filled with bunkbeds, each having a box to hold their personal belongings. Your personal space consists of your mattress, headphones, fan, television, and your box. Your box holds your most prized possessions — letters, photos, books, personal care items, snacks, and of course your prison currency, ramen noodles.

Other areas include "the hole" which is solitary confinement, even though the Indiana Department of Corrections does not like when I use that term. They tell me they do not participate in solitary confinement anymore. I don't know what else to call a cell where you are alone with a concrete bed, thin mattress, toilet, and smalltable, and not able to get out but for a few hours a week. This is where Dakota ultimately died.

In the winter prison is brutally cold and in the summer scorching hot. Showers are in an open room, as well as toilets. If your modesty is important to you, it won't be for long. Strip searches are very common. According to a grievance Dakota filed, it was common to be forced to be placed in a circle of men, made to strip, and be searched.

You must be prepared for a shake-down at a moment's notice. This is when guards come in and virtually uproot everything in the dorm, looking for contraband or other illegal things. They care little about the few items these people have, and will throw things around like it is trash, leaving it for the inmates to put it all back together.

Meals are not what most think. Society often believes that prisoners are fed better than those who live in a nursing home. I have knowledge of both and that is simply untrue. The average food cost for a nursing home resident ranges from six to eight dollars per day. The average food cost for an Indiana DOC inmate is approximately a little over a dollar. Most meals consist of a couple pieces of bread, lunch meat or peanut butter, and a cookie. Breakfast is at 4:00 a.m., lunch 11:00 a.m., and supper 4:00 p.m. Just because they are convicted of crimes does not mean that starving was part of the punishment.

The littlest gestures mean the most to those incarcerated. I had no idea how much my letters meant to Dakota. Many say there is no greater feeling than seeing the guard doing mail delivery and stopping by your bunk and throwing you a letter. They just want to know they are loved and haven't been forgotten. My family was amazing about writing to Dakota and letting him know he was still with us. They tell me the scent of home is on those letters. They would often fall asleep with those letters close to their head, just to be close to the person they miss so much.

The Indiana Department of Corrections publishes annual reports called "Fact Cards" and "Adult New Admission Reports." Those report that an average of twenty-five thousand inmates a year call prison home. Twenty percent of them are in maximum-security prisons. Of all the crimes committed, thirty-one percent are against people, twenty-five percent are related to controlled substances, and twelve percent against property. Ninety percent of them are male and sixty-two percent are white.

The Dearborn County prosecutor sent over fifteen hundred people to prison from 2013-2016. Through all his interviews after the *New York Times* article, he repeatedly states he is proud of his efforts. "Proud" would not be my choice of words when I know that I am destroying the lives of over fifteen hundred families. On the contrary, I would be searching for a solution to the problem my county was facing if my office was inundated with that much crime. In 2014, Dearborn County ranked third of ninety-two counties on prison admissions, and in 2015 ranked fifth. The only solution was aggressive prison sentences, which obviously did not work given the numbers of incarceration admissions year after year that he served. His plan of deterrence did not work. Instead, my family and countless others have been destroyed, not only by a substance abuse problem, but by what I feel is an abuse of power problem.

Going back to one of the goals of prison being rehabilitation, the prosecutor's greatest claim is that Dearborn County has a substance abuse program that criminals can attend. That is their handout to help those with substance abuse, then it's off to decades in prison.

Dakota attended that program and learned lots of information about substance abuse. The issue with this program is it is only ninety days. Most research shows that the rate of recovery after ninety days is less than twenty percent. Dakota was one of those statistics.

Dakota thought prison saved his life, and indeed it did for a time. I do believe that had he been given a just sentence, and been allowed a chance for his mind (which was not fully developed under the cloud of heroin) to clear, he could have been a contributing member of society. However, when you have over six decades of a prison sentence hanging over your head, I would have to think hope would slowly fade away.

Ultimately, depression in prison killed my son. I will spend the rest of my life speaking and advocating for a change in the system. What we permit, we promote. If we want to see change, we must be the change. This exact reason is why I am putting our story to print, knowing all too well the consequences I could potentially face, not just by people in my community, but more terrifyingly from those whom I am exposing, who possess great power in the legal system. But just like Esther in the Bible, perhaps I was born for such a time as this.

Naomi: A Mother's Broken Heart

Before Dakota's death, I prized my daily time reading my Bible and spending time with God. After he died, it took months for me to even open that beloved black leather-bound book I once cherished. One morning, I decided to finally open it again. I prayed heavily about where to even turn. In all honesty, I no longer believed a word printed on those thin white pages.

Something in my heart kept nudging me to read the Book of Ruth, although I didn't want to. Ruth had always been my favorite love story, but my heart was crushed to pieces, and the last thing I wanted was to read a love story. However, the feeling would not leave, so half-heartedly I started.

The first chapter was one I had always skimmed over before, because the love story starts in chapter two. This time chapter one drew me in like never before. I was introduced to a lady named Naomi. I had always known her just as Ruth's mother-in-law. Ruth has always been the main character to me, and I've read her story so many times I can almost recite it word for word. But this time, I met Naomi.

Chapter one introduces us to a biblical woman. It doesn't really give a lot of juicy details about her life, so I'm left to my own imagination. I love any story that starts with "once upon a time," a classic fairytale. We do know she followed her husband to a foreign land in search of food. There was a famine in the land, a crisis. I imagine her looking around her poverty-stricken town and feeling afraid. I imagine her looking at her young sons and knowing that without food, they will surely die. The love of a mother will push you out of your comfort zone. The love of a mother will cause you to fight with fierce determination. The love of a mother will cause you to do the impossible.

She trusted her man. She trusted he knew best, trusted he would never lead her wrong and always provide for her. She was on a journey of faith. She didn't have all the answers, but knew that where she was wasn't safe for her family. She was a wife and mother. She wanted to provide for her family. She knew staying in her comfortable home would result in the starvation and death of her children. They were fleeing from poverty and danger, and so was I.

Once they arrived, it was time to get adjusted. I imagine her settling into their new home, watching over her young adult sons and husband. I wonder what she dreamed of. I wonder if she was making new friends in town. She appeared to be living a safe and secure life, far from the life she left.

Then all at once, her safe and secure home toppled upside down. She suffered the loss of her husband. I wonder how he died. Was he sick? Or did she just get a knock at the door one day and learn he'd been in an accident? I'm sure he was the love of her life, her security. He brought her here to this foreign land in search for a brighter future, and now he was gone. I can see her in her black widow's dress, veil and sunglasses, standing next to a grave mourning her husband and best friend.

However, he might have been gone but he did leave her a legacy, the sacred gift of her sons. He left her with a retirement plan, to ensure her years be secure. Despite dealing with the broken heart of losing the love of her life, she still had her family. She still had a reason to get out of bed every morning. She still had her faith.

Eventually her young sons found wives. Unfortunately, these daughters-in-law were not girls from her heritage and bloodline. I wonder if she approved of those girls. Did they measure up to her standards? Nevertheless, I imagine her participating in the wedding planning, picking flowers, and planning a guest list. I also can see her with tears in her eyes as those wedding vows are exchanged, knowing her boys are now officially men, men who now belong to another woman. I can only envision how she felt God had blessed, secured and made her life comfortable again, despite her still grieving hard over the loss of her husband. I'm certain she was so grateful her sons wouldn't have to deal with the struggles of where they came from, just like me.

The story is vague with the details, yet it's written that within the next ten years she lost not one but both sons. She was alone, no sons and no husband in a foreign land.

Knowing the pain of losing one son, I simply can't wrap my mind about the emotions Naomi must have felt.

I've spoken to widows who feel angry that their spouse unexpectedly left them. They speak of retirement plans filled with travel. I've spoken with countless other mothers who have buried a child, each with that hollow look in their eyes and each muttering the same thing: "A mother isn't supposed to bury their child. It's supposed to be the other way around." Each of these women say the same final sentence, as I have so many times, "This was not the way the story was supposed to end." I'm sure Naomi felt the same way.

My heart holds a special place for Naomi. So many of us are struggling to muster the energy to live after the devastation of one death, much less three. She was still grieving the loss of her husband, but now had to deal with not only the shock over the death of one son, but two. She agonized with not being able to say goodbye and hug her loved ones, not once, but three times.She donned her grieving gown, not once, but three times. She watched a casket be lowered into the cold dark ground, not once, but three times. Everything single thing she held close and cherished was ripped from her.

After experiencing my grief and anger toward God, I can't help but to think of her feelings of anger, sadness, and fear. She literally lost everything in ten years, everything! I imagine she sat alone many times screaming at God, "Why me? Why my husband? Why my sons? Why are you taking everything from me? Why are you doing this to me?" Just like I have a thousand times.

There's nothing in the Book of Ruth that portrays the days, months or years of her grief journey. She doesn't describe her counseling sessions, books she read, crying sessions with her girlfriends, or the days she couldn't pull herself out of her bed with its tear-stained pillowcases. Instead, the story goes on to tell how she pulled herself together (Ruth 1:6). One day, she realized she was still living and somehow must go on. She must dream again. She made the decision that it was time to go home to her family. She was tired of being alone. She needed to go back.

She had one problem, however. She had two daughters-in-law. She tried to get them to stay and not follow her back. She tried to get them to understand she barely had the energy to take care of herself, much less them. She was having a hard enough time just to keep herself in the lifeboat, much less be responsible for their survival, too. She knew they could go back to their mothers.

I imagine her hugging them a final goodbye, something she'd become so accustomed to. I imagine her grasping those sweet girls' faces and trying to help them see their future. They can find love again; they're young. They could build a life, home and family, everything she had lost. She had lost all hope. She was trying to get the girls to see the brighter future that she could not. She was so bitter, and she was so open in her pain. She blamed God.

Only one problem — Ruth refused to leave her. During that final hug, Ruth wouldn't let go. Despite all Naomi tried to tell her, Ruth wasn't budging. Ruth begged Naomi to not make her leave her, to not send her back. Her exact words to Naomi were, "Don't force me to leave you; don't make me go home. Where you go, I go; and where you live, I'll live. Your people are my people, your God is my god; where you die, I'll die, and that's where I'll be buried, so help me God-not even death itself is going to come between us!" (Ruth 1:16-17)

The beautiful part of this story is God knows we cannot survive the grieving process alone. He sends people to come alongside us and refuse to leave. I've been so blessed to have friends and family who refuse to leave me. So many people have called to just sit and cry with me. Family surrounded me countless times on my porch and graciously listened to my tales of memories. My husband has dried enough tears to water a garden. I've been showered with gifts to constantly remind me that like Naomi, I wasn't alone.

One of those gifts was a book from our dear friend Alice. I'm ashamed to say that it took me a year to even open the book. Just the title, *I Wasn't Ready to Say Goodbye* (by Brook Noel and Pamela D. Blair), paralyzed me for months. Seeing that book and allowing myself to open the cover was like saying I *was* ready; but I was far from ready to say goodbye, nor would I ever be. Like Naomi, I was bitter! She felt God was dealing harshly with her. (Ruth 1:20-21) She was depleted and depressed. She lost everything. She felt ruined; so did I.

The painful picture of grief, I was struggling to muster the energy to roll out of bed and go to work. Once I arrived home, I was drowning my pain in a bottle of white wine and not moving from my patio chair. I was bitter. I felt God was heaping on too much for me to bear. I was severely exhausted and severely miserable. I had lost the first love of my life. I was ruined and I felt like my life was slowly ending. And I wanted it to. So many times, I would drive home and think, *God, You allowed him to die; why won't You allow me?* I would go to bed at night and beg to die in my sleep, only to be so angry the next morning when I woke up.

Reading Ruth, I finally felt like I met someone who could understand what I was experiencing, the pain I felt and the dark pit I couldn't crawl out of. I became best friends with Naomi. I spent the next few weeks with her. I read all her story, written so beautifully in the Bible. I put into place everything she did. She let others provide for her, and so did I. She let those close to her love her, and so did I. She shared her experience and feelings with others, and so did I. She kept her faith in God and his goodness, and so did I, even if mine was thin and shredded. She believed God still loved her in good times and bad, and so did I. She believed in redemption, and so did I.

Her tragedy was the set-up to a comeback, in her legacy as great-great-grandmother to King David, and ultimately, the lineage of Jesus. My legacy isn't over, and my tragedy will be used for God's glory, just like Naomi. But perhaps Naomi should've added a little antidepressant medication like me. I wish I could say that grieving has a well-written process with outlined steps. It doesn't. The best I've seen it described is as waves. Some days you think you're growing out of the anger into another stage. For me, right now, I seem to float between anger and guilt.

Pain is a powerful emotion. It's crippling if you allow it to steal your energy, your ability to think, your hopes and dreams. For me, pain is the only emotion I can experience. Everyone kept wanting to share their memories of Dakota, and I couldn't remember anything before the day he took his life. I felt like I was literally losing my mind. I had lost him and now I was losing my precious memories. If I would look at pictures that should invoke a feeling of joy, all I could feel was hurt. The memories used to be sweet and now they were too painful to remember.

I was immersed in the life of a drug addict. Remember, I was taught early on that most use substances to feel something or not to feel something. I wanted the pain to stop. I begged for God to numb the hurt. I finally understood the reason behind suicide. I used to think it was so selfish. Now I understand that when all hope for a better tomorrow is extinguished, and the pain is beyond numbing, Satan sneaks in to whisper a way out. Suicide.

One night I went to bed, after praying day after day for God to reveal to me the details of that day. Dakota's death haunted me. I could not and still cannot stop thinking about what he was thinking that day. When he woke up and went to chow, did he know this would be his last meal? What did he eat? Did he replay every wonderful memory of his life? What did his prayers sound like? What was he thinking about me as his mother? Did I do enough? Did he know my love was genuine and beyond words to describe? Did he know I loved him beyond depths of my soul I had never explored? What was he saying to his brother in his thoughts? Was he scared? When he was dying, did he feel pain? Did he linger for those two hours, or was it a sudden last breath on Earth and instant arrival in Heaven? Who did he get the fentanyl from? How did he get it?

Finally, one night God blessed me with the most amazing dream. Dakota hadn't appeared in my dreams prior and hasn't again since that night. I dreamed I was in the cell with him. I was sitting on a chair in the corner on the far-right side. I never said a word. Dakota was sitting on his bunk, elbows on his knees, holding something in his hands. He never looked at me, but just kept staring at what was in his hands. The cell was cold, dingy, and gray, yet I remember feeling the most peace I had felt in a long time.

Finally Dakota said without looking at me, "Mom, I can't do this for the rest of my life. In one hour, this will all be over for me." And there I sat with the eeriest peace I've felt in years. I understood, even if it would shatter my heart, that I would surrender my broken heart to save his precious soul. It's the strangest sense of peace because normally I would've been jumping up, grabbing him and hugging him, screaming, "No, please don't leave me!" But I know I got to go home after every visit. He was humiliated and stripped of every ounce of dignity and pride, just to enjoy a one-hour visit of frozen bacon cheeseburgers, Yoo-hoo, Nestle cookie crunch bar and a bag of Doritos with me.

He woke up every single day to the loud disruption of a prison. His personal space consisted of open dorms with his bunk bed and trunks. His personal prized possessions were a TV with headphones, a fan, and his "box" where he would keep his commissary. He had no freedom over choosing the simplest of things. He would never get to experience Christmas morning at home again, or his favorite holiday, Thanksgiving. He would never marry, have children or a home. He knew that when I died, he would never be given the opportunity to attend my funeral and say goodbye.

I used to believe that anyone who committed suicide would never be welcomed into Heaven. That was official doctrine that had been crammed down my throat from the time I was a little girl. I've since scoured the scripture and have been unable to find that written in my Bible. Based on the lantern, my dream, Dakota's personal writings and the word of God, I confidently believe without a doubt that he's waiting for me in Heaven. I truly believe God had to break my heart to save Dakota's soul. I also believe that if one of us had to die first, I'm glad it was him instead of me. I would never wish this kind of grieving on him to go through alone, behind bars. I get to visit his grave; he would not have been able to visit mine.

I've finally stopped asking God "why?" I've realized that God, too, knows what the grieving heart of a parent feels like. He knows what it feels like to have a son indicted, stripped, robbed of his dignity, labeled, and murdered. He knows how it feels to have to stand by and do nothing while evil destroys a child. The difference between our sons is His was innocent and mine wasn't. I've learned the "why" is associated with free will. As painful as it is, the life Dakota lived, from heroin to crime, was a result of his free will, not God's doing.

As requested by my brother, I've learned to not allow sadness to become my new default emotion, despite how easy that would be. I refuse to allow Dakota's drug addiction, crime and death to define him or me, or to change who I am or my identity in Christ. Satan wants nothing more than to know that all God invested in you was for nothing. He wants you to believe the lie of no hope and no faith.

The light at the end of my tunnel of grief is relying on Joel 2:25. Basically, the Lord says, "I will give you back what you lost." I do know that I've temporarily lost contact with Dakota in the natural, but I know that when my assignment is over I will hug him again. I do believe that the other things I've lost, such as joy, laughter, energy, the ability to dream, will be restored as Joel 2:25 promises. Trials cause you to grow. You ultimately must choose to grow bitter or better. I choose better, even if I don't feel it.

Every single day remains a fight for me to choose to live, to choose to still look for small viable signs of life. The tears continue to flow, and my heart still breaks every day. I'm still navigating my new normal. I still play "Even If" by MercyMe almost daily. I'm still angry and sad. I still question why this had to be our story. I still miss my son like crazy. I still love him and am proud to be his mom.

I always said I hated the phrase "drug addict," and now I add "committed suicide" to that list. Those aren't accurate labels. The victims of addiction and suicide are beautiful souls who belong to God. They've experienced an amount of pain that to them was unbearable, and those options were the only means of escape. God loves them just as much as you and me.

Mary

I'd like to introduce you to another shero of mine, Mary. I've read her story countless times, and until you're going through similar situations you can only feel sympathy, not empathy. With the passing of my son, I was urged to revisit her story. If I could have called her on the phone I would have. I love to imagine sitting across the table from her with a cup of coffee. My first question would be, "What went through your mind when you found out you were pregnant, young and unmarried? Were you afraid Joseph would leave when he found out? How did that conversation start out? What was it like to raise Jesus, who often went about things his own way and not yours? Please tell me how you survived his death? How could you forgive those who did the unthinkable to him? When does this ache ever go away?"

Her story begins in the Book of Matthew. Mary was the most unlikely woman to be chosen to birth and mother the Savior of the World. She was young and unmarried, just like me; I was barely eighteen and unmarried when I had Dakota. I'm sure she had dreams for her future that didn't include ridicule, doubt, and being tasked to raise the Son of God. I did too; I wanted to go to college and be a nurse.

As I read her story, I go back to what she must have felt when she was chosen for such a huge purpose. I'm sure she held that child, like I did, and thought, *Oh my goodness, I'm totally responsible for another human being, not just myself!* Someone had to mother this child; so did I. Why did God choose her? Why did God choose me? She was unmarried! Why did he choose someone who would cause everyone to doubt her story? In my imagination, I can see all the girls in town gossiping about how they think she really got pregnant, like they did me. How could anyone believe a virgin conceiving a child? That was absolutely and utterly impossible.

I imagine the whispers and shuns as she conducted her day-to-day business. Can you imagine trying to explain this miracle to Joseph, much less those who did not know her? I can hear the whispers and accusations of the other women in town, gossiping and making assumptions about her situation.

I'm sure Mary asked a thousand times, like I did, "God, why did You choose me? Why are You allowing this to happen to my son? Why are You allowing my family to go through this? Perhaps it was because I wasn't a perfect mother; after all, I did misplace my son at twelve years old." (Luke 2:43) All I can come up with is that it was training for the trials that were about to come. God knew her strength and faith, like mine (even though I had no idea until I was forced to exercise it). God knew she had broad enough shoulders to weather the storm of gossip and scorn of an unwed pregnancy, like me. God knew she had the courage to raise this child, even if she would ultimately have to do it alone, like me. She would be strong enough to stand tall in the mockery of her son and ultimately his death, like me. He trusted her with His most prized possession, His Son.

In the Books of Matthew, Mark and Luke, we see how she follows her son on a journey that included ridicule, torture, and death. She never left. She heard his friends betray him. She had to stand by helplessly and watch her son be hit in the head with a club. She felt each sting as her son was whipped with strips of leather on his bare skin. She felt humility when she watched them strip him naked and mock him. She turned her head every time they spat in his face. She stood behind her son while they mocked, accused, made fun of and ultimately sentenced her son to death. I know all too well the sting of the tears that were streaming down her face. I have felt the heaviness of her chest from holding her breath, hoping this was all just a bad dream.

She watched as he stood before his accusers and humbly said nothing to defend himself. She saw him struggle to carry his own cross. She sat in horror as they lifted his badly beaten and bruised body to the cross. With each strike of the hammer, she could feel the pierce of the nails that entered first one hand and then the other. I imagine by the time they got to nailing his feet, her anguish was overwhelming. I can feel her total emotional breakdown.

It began at nine o'clock in the morning. She watched her now grown man of a son hang in extreme torture and humility for three long and agonizing hours. I can only imagine she was begging God to please just make this stop. Finally, his human body couldn't take one more minute of the pain pulsating through him, and he screamed out, "My God, My God, why have you abandoned me?" (Matthew 27: 45-46). For another three hours she sat, helpless, watching her son die a slow torturous death that he didn't deserve. At last, he inhaled his final breath. It was over for him; but for her, grief was just fully beginning.

The Bible says once everyone left, she stayed (Matthew 27:57-61). What was she thinking? Was she remembering the day he was born, being given her son swaddled in blankets? She had no idea that thirty-three years later she would witness the horrific scene of her son's death. I'm sure she replayed every memory of his teen years leading into his adult life. She had to be mourning the loss of every dream she had of the things he would accomplish. I'm certain that, just as I did, she sat alone at the tomb and screamed at the top of her lungs, "Why, God, why? This was not the way the story was supposed to end!"

I'm projecting my own grief story on Mary, even though our sons are vastly different. Her son was innocent in every way. Mine was guilty in more ways than one. We share a similar story of being left to grieve the death of our boys. In a way, I've been slowly grieving the loss of Dakota for seven long years. However, death is final. There is no hope for a turnaround story. For the decedent, their pain is over. For the surviving, especially a parent, it's a life sentence never to be escaped, a prison one can never leave.

The grieving cycle isn't wrapped up in a pretty little box with assigned time cycles. Grief is messy. It is ugly. Just like heroin, it causes you to speak and act in ways you would not normally do. Anger commonly seems to be the first emotion. I was, and still am, angry! I was angry at Dakota for making the choices that caused all this, and for ultimately not giving me the chance to say goodbye. I just would've told him I understood, and that being his mother was the greatest thing that has ever happened to me. I would've told him I am so proud of him. Lastly, I would've promised him that as long as I have breath in my lungs, he will never be forgotten.

I was angry at his friends for introducing him to this lifestyle and then so easily walking away. I was angry at the people who participated in those final acts, who received a slap on the wrist, and now act as if Dakota never existed. He would've died for them, and in a way he did.

I was angry that drug addiction is still such a dirty secret no one wants to talk about, and that our form of "treatment" is incarceration.

I was angry at a justice system that could've given him a harsh sentence and taught him a lesson, without it being over six decades. Justice wasn't served, but a life sentence was.

Most importantly, I was angry at myself. I've replayed things over and over and over in my mind of what I could've done differently, beginning on November 16, 1993.

Then comes surrender. Eventually you must stop asking "why" questions. There are some things we will never understand on this side of Heaven. In my case, I'll never know what the final straw was that caused Dakota to give up and die by suicide. All I know is he must've lost his last little glimmer of hope of ever walking out those gates at Pendleton. I know that he didn't want to die; he just wanted to end his immense pain. His life was hell. I wouldn't selfishly wish him back one day. Especially when I know that he's now in paradise.

Then comes forgiveness. You must forgive. It's a decision, not an emotion. You need to sit down and be honest with yourself. Ask God to show you everyone in your heart you need to forgive. Make a list of everyone who comes to mind. Forgiveness doesn't resolve them of what they did, nor do you have to invite them back into your life. Unforgiveness hurts only yourself. Clear that space in your heart. It's like cancer and serves you no good purpose. Open that space in your heart to love. Look for people around you who are going through what you went through. Use that energy to shower them with love and compassion. Turn your test into your testimony.

Ride the emotional rollercoaster. You will be your own worst enemy. Dealing with suicide or the death of a child are each devastating losses. After Dakota died, my entire body seemed to shut down. My memory faded. My energy depleted. I either slept too much or not enough. My patience for people was spent. Then the nurse in me reminded myself it's almost like being in the ICU. I just experienced a traumatic event. I needed to love myself and care for myself just like I would a patient in intensive care. It's been a year and half and I'm still riding the rollercoaster. Some days it feels like three steps forward and five steps back. I know this will be a lifelong journey for me. I've found that using my story to help others is the best medicine I can take.

Pain can be a very dangerous tool. Just like it caused Dakota to die, if not careful I could've allowed it to take me out as well. I strongly recommend counseling and immediate help for anyone struggling with thoughts of suicide. Find healthy ways to deal with the pain. I turned to wine to numb the pain, but unfortunately you wake up in the morning with it all right there ready to greet you again, except now you have a terrible hangover to deal with, too. Substances of any type are only a Band-Aid to the problem, not the solution.

Choose to be happy. Happiness is a choice. You must choose to be happy even when you don't feel like it. You can't control the death of a child, but you can control how you choose to move forward. You can turn a mess into a message.

Grief is a process. I hate to tell you this, but you'll never entirely get over it. I'm in no way an expert, as I'm still working through my own journey, but I recommend you find what works for you. There are great support groups, you can lean on family and friends, take medication if it helps, go for daily walks, journal, seek professional help, read books. You are not in this alone.

As for me, I'm choosing to live my best life ever (I promise, Dakota), even when I don't feel like it or know what that even looks like.

Now It's Dakota's Turn

First off, I would like to go ahead and apologize to everybody affected by my actions, most importantly the victims. I'm sorry I took your sense of security when I came into your houses. I know my apologies cannot make things right and specifically it's not your place. I wish I could go back in time and fix this. There are no excuses for what I have done. If I'm given an opportunity to make things right, I'll pay you back to the fullest extent, and I know I'm going to have a long time to think about the things that I have done. I hope that you guys can regain your sense of security, and try to move forward in your lives and put this experience behind you. I'm sorry that you guys have been burdened by this.

To my family I would like to apologize for making poor choices in life to get me where I am. We all know that I was raised better than this. I know I've let all you guys down by either stealing, lying or anything else I've done in the past six years in my addiction. I'm sorry I've chose this direction in life and made such a bad reputation for myself, which is falling back on my family.

Mom, I'm sorry that you feel guilty for the choices I've made, and I hope you can finally think that you did your best to raise me, and my actions are what got me here and there's no one to blame but myself. I'm sorry for the emotional burden that I've caused to help my addiction, also the financial burden to try to support me through all of this.

Terri, I know it's been rough, but you've been with me through this, you stuck by my side and have been one of my biggest supporters no matter what. I'm sorry that I let you down. You trusted me with Michelle, and I wasn't smart enough to stay away from dope. I'm sorry you guys out there have to go through this because of my choices.

Also, I would like to apologize, even my girlfriend's not here, to her because I do owe her an apology for the fact that she's in prison paying for choices that I made. She played a minor role in these burglaries. I don't remember when I got so bad, but I wish I could have been stronger to keep me and her from getting on dope again or somehow prevented this.

To my little brothers, I'm sorry I haven't been the role model you guys needed and I hope that you guys can learn through my mistakes. And also, everyone else, all my friends and family that I've let down, I appreciate all you guys' support and I'm sorry for letting you guys down.

And Your Honor, I'm sorry I've wasted the Court's valuable time and took so long to come to a resolution. I'm sure people tell you all the time that they do things because of dope and that there are no excuses for it, and I shouldn't just blame it on dope. What I've done and just because of dope, I made the choices to do it but throughout my addiction. I would have cut off my arm and gave it to a drug dealer if they would have given me heroin for it.

All these things that I took from these homes went toward heroin. Me and my girlfriend were using four to six hundred dollars a day on heroin. It does not make these things right what I did but I know if I was given the tools to overcome my addiction, I could become a productive member of society and work a regular job and support myself.

Before, I never put much effort into rehabilitation, because I was young and I was dumb, and I have not really lost anything to heroin. It took me a long time to realize it, but I finally realized the effects of heroin. It has ruined my life in so many ways. It's taken my pride. I'm known as a drug addict and a thief. I burned bridges with people that I wish I wouldn't have. I bit the hand that fed me.

My whole life, the only person that has always stood by my side, my mom. I stole jewelry out of her jewelry box, sentimental things like her dead father's wedding band, and I know that those things can't be replaced. I don't know anyone that likes a liar or thief, but on heroin that's all I am. I only have but a couple of friends left that have now stopped associating with me because of heroin. I practically lost my girlfriend due to heroin, one of the most important aspects of my life, and now I'm also going to be using years of my life doing time.

It took all the way up until a year ago to finally realize I absolutely hate everything about heroin, but at the end of the day I chose to do heroin. If I could take it back, I would. But once you do it, it's like you sell yourself to the devil. That stuff sucked the life out of me, and I also realize the ripple effect that not only heroin had an effect on me but also my family and my community and so on and so on.

I'm not going to lie and tell you I have some plan to stay sober. Honestly, I've been so focused on trying to figure out how I'm going to have a chance to get back into a society that I haven't really even thought about getting out.

I know that just being released from prison with no type of re-entry is so overwhelming for me, I know I have to have a slow process out. I've never had house arrest or anything intensive. I've just been released to probation and something like that I think would help me, because I need more help than just myself, and while I'm in prison I'm going to try to get a college degree and program and work on becoming a productive member of society.

My attitude and outlook on life has changed a lot in eighteen months. I'm starting to grow up. I'm starting to get my priorities in order. I'm still working on myself, though, and I still got a long way to go. I just keep hope and try to stay positive no matter what.

I was twenty years old when I did these, and I know I have to pay for my crimes. I'm just asking you not to give up on me. I do want to be a productive person. I've taken from my community enough and I'd like to be able to give back in a positive way. I want to have an opportunity to start a family and a career, and be able to overcome my addiction and try to help others, and not make the same bad choices I have.

Me getting caught for these crimes is probably the only thing that saved my life. This last nineteen months has been the most humbling experience of my life, and me taking responsibility for these actions is the first step to change my life, facing my past so I can get past it and focus on coming home a better person and live a normal life.

Once again, I'm sorry to everybody that these crimes affected.

Redemption

When I replay the dramatic twists and turns of our story in my mind, or when I have a captive listener who's interested in hearing it, I'm still amazed at how a sweet innocent boy could make such terrible decisions, ones that had such a costly outcome and altered the course of his life forever. I'm still in shock that I'm among the membership of sisters who have lost a child, not only to addiction, but also to suicide.

It all takes me back to the story in the Bible found in Luke 15, starting in verse 11, of the prodigal son (interpretation my own). It's the story of a father who had two sons. Both sons were set to receive an inheritance. The younger son was impulsive and impatient, and wanted his inheritance now. I'm sure Dad knew that too much too soon would have disastrous results, yet he allowed the young boy to receive the inheritance and do all his heart desired. I imagine the heartbreak Dad must have been feeling, knowing that a young man without life experience with that much money would only lead to trouble. I'm certain tears strolled down his cheeks as he watched his son leave. I can see his pillowcase stained with tears from many nights of lying in bed wondering where his son was. Was he happy? Was he safe? Did he do the right thing?

The son, on the contrary, had money in his pocket, packed his bags as quickly as he could, and left home. He was living a lavish lifestyle, entertaining friends in penthouse suites with different women every night. His closets were filled with the most polished clothing, and he had the sweetest new ride on the lot. Every single night, he feasted on steak and lobster. I see the empty top-shelf liquor bottles laying all over the room. There lie mirrors, razor blades and white powdery substances. In the corner, in my eye I see a young handsome man sitting on the edge of the bed with a brown belt wrapped around his left arm, with a needle in his right hand ready to start "the party."

He hated everything about his small town, and now he was in a new place, enjoying the benefits of his inheritance. He experienced indulgence, trading his destiny for minutes of gratification. What he didn't plan for was the fact that every decision has consequences, either beneficial or detrimental. You can only run in a certain direction for so long before you must face the curse or enjoy the blessing.

Eventually the money ran out; and without money, there was no hotels, booze, drugs, girls, fancy dinners, cars, clothes. When he realized he was down to nothing, his "friends" quickly left and betrayed him. Perhaps he began committing petty crimes to satisfy his craving, to keep up his lifestyle. As with every addict, it would only be a matter of time before the prodigal son too would have a demonic addiction and criminal record, and eventually be homeless and hungry. He went from having everything to nothing. He had ruined every shred of life he once had. His dignity was gone, his reputation tarnished.

He had finally reached his bottom. He had dropped to his knees. Verses 12 through 16 show us his pain. He was hurting and hungry. He was homeless, begging for food, and no one would even look in his direction. That was his surrender point. He remembered home. He wondered what his family was doing. I imagine he had images of his father, brother, and mother having dinner around the kitchen table. Did they remember him? Did they miss him? Were they worried about him? Did they even think of him at all? Would they forgive him?

While he was hustling for his next high or scraping for his next meal, he recalled the warmth of his bed and his family. He wanted to return home. Would they accept him? Would they reject him? It was a risk he was willing to take. I imagine him humbly packing his few belongings. Maybe he had track marks on his arms. Maybe he was dope sick with nausea, vomiting, diarrhea, and leg tremors, unable to sleep. Yet he longed for home; so he packed up his belongings, his pride and his shame, and started home.

I imagine his father in the yard working hard, and looking up to see his estranged son walking down the drive. Broke, worn down, strung out on a party lifestyle, and humbly coming home. How would his father respond? Perhaps angry that his son had squandered every penny he had been given? Embarrassed with what the family friends would say? Would his father turn his head and teach him tough love?

On the contrary, that father ran down the long drive to hug his lost son. The boy was so ashamed. He kept repeating every bad thing he had done. He wasn't expecting to be welcomed back; he just wanted to be in their presence. Dad wasn't listening, but instead just kept hugging and kissing his son. Happiness and relief weren't enough to describe his emotions! He ordered an immediate celebration. *Get this boy some clean clothes, start the grill, and thaw out the best steaks. Our son is home!* Dad just kept telling the son how worried he had been, thinking he was dead or never coming home. And here he was, finally home!

I imagine that's what God feels for us. Like the prodigal son's father, I too know the feeling of Dakota walking through the door after having messed up too many times to count. I know the joy of hope from him returning from rehab, feeling like this time will be the change. I know the feeling of unconditional love, despite the loss of things stolen that could never be replaced. I would've laid my life down a thousand and one times for my son. This leads me to only ask that if my earthly love can extend this far, how much more does an unfailing, unwavering God love us, and love my Dakota?

Dakota was a young man with his entire life ahead of him. He was destined for college, a career, family, and a future. He made a choice — a choice to stick a needle filled with heroin in his veins. He bought into a lie, a few minutes of ecstasy in exchange for his destiny. His inheritance was quickly spent on legal fees which eventually ran dry.

Courts didn't give Dakota justice, yet God gave him redemption. Redemption is defined as being saved from something in exchange for something. Again, I believe that God broke my heart to save Dakota's soul. That's a high price for any mother to pay, but the reward is the greatest gift a mother could receive.

One early morning I was sitting on my deck when it dawned on me that out of all the worries of the world, nothing compares to the comfort of knowing that when you die you will meet your children in Heaven. That immediately downplays any worry you're facing in the earthly realm. In all reality, this isn't an end, just the beginning. Jesus ultimately paid the price for Dakota's freedom, a price that no amount of my money could buy. I have learned that often God won't change your circumstances, so that He can instead change your heart.

I wanted, and tried desperately, to take care of and make all of Dakota's problems and legal issues go away. All my efforts seemed to come to nothing. Dakota needed God, not me. Dakota needed salvation, not earthly freedom, all of which was only possible through grace and mercy, not Mom's checkbook. That's when I had to make that hard decision to surrender on our appeal to the Supreme Court. We both needed to trust God to write the final chapter.

God's greatest power is revealed through our broken stories. I've learned that mercy is relief from the punishment we deserve, and grace is the power of God working through our lives. Disaster often must occur in our lives for us to see or appreciate these two amazing attributes of God. I know it did mine. He will often take the broken pieces of your life, what Satan used to hurt you, and use those to let His glory shine the brightest.

It's the brutality of the cross that shows the beauty of redemption. I often think of those three crosses on Calvary, our Savior in the middle, as we're taught in Sunday school to focus on. However, my eyes travel to the two guys on both sides of an innocent man, criminals. They both have committed the most heinous crimes for reasons unknown to us. Society is ready to watch them suffer the most horrific death. They have left victims in the wake of their crimes. Yet, Jesus!

In those times, my son would be hung on a cross and beaten for his crimes. I imagine nails being pierced through those precious hands and feet that only twenty-four years ago I kissed, admired and counted every finger and toe of. In society's eyes, he was evil and deserved death. Yet in my eyes, he was one of the most precious souls who ever walked the face of this earth. There he was, hanging on a cross next to my Savior.

With the greatest love and compassion, I imagine Jesus looking over at my baby. Blood streams down Jesus' precious, innocent face, as He tells Dakota, "This was all for you! I came to walk this earth to feel your pain. I preach of my Father's love and mercy to all who would listen. I survived this torture, and went to the depths of Hell, just for you, my precious son. You, Dakota, will meet me in paradise. Sin is cancelled by grace, which is redemption."

I imagine that sweet son of mine saying, "Jesus, you don't know what I've done. I've lied, cheated, and stolen from innocent people. I've kicked in doors. I've broken my mother's heart. Even when I want to do the right thing, I still choose the wrong thing. I'm not worthy of going to Heaven. I'm worthy of a life sentence in Hell to pay for my actions, like the prosecutor said."

I further picture Jesus responding with, "Dakota, I have already paid your restitution, $42,556 and life in prison, with my blood. Welcome home! It is finished."

I can only imagine the conversations taking place in Hell at this time. Satan thought he had won. My grandmother prophesied over Dakota when he was born that he was destined for greatness. I think Satan saw the future God had planned for Dakota and went on the attack. Dakota fell into his trap and bought his lies, especially that he wouldn't live past twenty-five, which he didn't. Satan thought he had won. I am sure Queen's "Another One Bites the Dust" was blaring in Hell. But God!

Your past does not define you or your future. God chose you as a cherished treasure, out of His sheer love. He knew all the screw-ups you would ever have. Deuteronomy 7:7-10 states His "love for you has nothing to do with you, only his sheer love for you and his promise to your ancestors," perhaps your mom, like He did me with Luke 1:45. He steps in and pulls you out of slavery, which in my son's case was drug addiction; but perhaps for you it's alcohol, pornography, gambling, etc.

Repentance

Redemption isn't free. The price of sin is high. As humans, we're given free will. I believe we're all born with an intuition of right or wrong. We're free to choose. However, don't get it twisted; our choice will have a price.

For Dakota, he chose his friends. He chose to do heroin. He chose crime to feed an addiction. We all like to judge people and say, "Well, at least I don't steal." "At least I don't do drugs." "At least I haven't killed anyone." Yet if I was to ask you if you've talked negatively about someone; not forgiven someone who has done you wrong; cheated on your taxes; didn't take back that item that didn't ring up at that grocery and that you walked out with; stayed a little over on the clock; had just a few drinks and drove home; flirted with that person at work despite that circular band on your left ring finger. All those things are wrong; yet since they're just "little" wrongs, socially acceptable wrongs, we somehow feel morally that we can sit in the judgement seat of others.

Dakota's criminal actions all started with just an "innocent" choice to fit in, a choice that spiraled out of control. A choice that became bigger than him. A choice that cost him his freedom and ultimately his life. Your choices, too, will have consequences, just perhaps not a life sentence in prison, to be played on the media for the world to see. Despite that, I promise you will have to pay the costs.

I chose to support my son through this journey, despite what people thought. I choose what I believed was best, even if it proved to be wrong. I chose the course of treatment, even if it failed. I chose the attorneys, even if they didn't take their job seriously. I chose to trust the judicial system, even if it was unjust. I chose honesty over deceit, even if it didn't turn out like I had hoped. It all came with a price to pay, a serious price I will pay for the rest of my life.

As I mentioned earlier, decisions have consequences, and I eventually had to stop blaming God. Please don't misunderstand me. I'm not saying every bad thing that happens to people is a result of sin. Cancer in a young child isn't due to their sin. The death of a father in a car crash doesn't mean he sinned. A mother diagnosed with breast cancer and dying, leaving small children, isn't the price of sin.

There are plenty of tragic things that happen to people where their actions by no means caused them to happen. I am not God. I cannot explain why bad things happen to good people. What I can say is that everyone has a story to tell of survival. Tell your story; it will help others. Only you can choose whether you allow your story to make you better or bitter.

I'm speaking from the world of addiction, crime, and human choice. I have a friend who also had a daughter in prison as a result of drug addiction. She's told me numerous times, "I wish I could get to where you are...I wish I wouldn't be angry at my daughter...I wish I could support my daughter like you do, but I can't. I'm frustrated, angry, and hurt." She's also been left to raise three small granddaughters due to her daughter's incarceration.

I remind her often that our stories are different. Trust me, I've felt severe anger toward Dakota over his actions. I've felt so frustrated as to why he kept going back to a dirty needle. I've laid in a fetal position in my bed and begged God to just take this away from me, as I simply couldn't carry this anymore. I've felt rage over looking back at Derick's childhood and all he lost. I've suffered severe shame in my community, knowing the things Dakota's actions took from others.

Regardless, at the end of the day, my love for my son conquered all. There is no greater feeling than love. Love truly covers a multitude of sins.

Keep in mind, sin is not a solo activity. No one can get through life without their actions affecting others. It's often a family affair. Drug addiction has destroyed my life, yet I've never experienced the first high. Why I am so passionate about this? According to the Annie E. Casey Foundation's Kids Count Data Center in Indiana, 48 percent of children live in single-parent homes. Ten percent of children have a parent incarcerated.

Think about that for a second. These are our neighbors. Your kids go to school with these kids. Single-parent homes and incarcerated parents place kids at higher risk of drug addiction and incarceration themselves. Next time you're outside, look around at those sweet faces. Which one of those kids would you be okay with knowing that they got addicted to drugs and are heading to prison?

Remember what my students taught me. Everyone uses drugs to feel something or to not feel something. No one can ever convince me that the four of ten kids playing in your yard who are only getting to see their daddy every other weekend aren't feeling pain. Furthermore, one of those ten kids in your yard only gets to see their parent on rare occasions because they're incarcerated.

Indiana University's Addictions website states that one in ten young people have taken prescription pain medication not prescribed to them in the past year. Children with a parent who is addicted to drugs are four times more likely to abuse drugs as well. According to a study from the Substance Abuse and Mental Health Services Administration, one in five people over the age of twelve — read that again, twelve years old — used a substance during the last year. Yet only one percent received treatment. Their drug of choice to start with is usually marijuana, with the second most abused being prescription pain pills they often obtain from a friend or family member. Also noteworthy, depression numbers correlate with the number of kids abusing drugs.

According to the State of Indiana's website, nine out of ten people with addiction began using before the age of eighteen. *Nine out of ten*! We think of drug addicts as old, dirty junkies. Those "junkies" were someone's precious teen when they first started abusing drugs or alcohol. Drug addiction isn't just a problem among poor people who live in the projects. It knows no socioeconomic boundaries. You're no different than me. In a blink of an eye, you could be writing this story.

I could go on and on about statistics to paint a picture. Remember, I completed a year of study and a thesis on Adolescence and Opiate Abuse. The numbers are clear and a bitter pill for me to swallow. I was a single mother of two boys. I thought I could do just as good on my own as a two-parent family does. I thought Dakota experimenting with marijuana was a typical teenage thing. I wanted to believe that the young men Dakota was associating with were great influences. I never imagined Dakota's father's incarceration would impact his life and glamorize incarceration. Everything the prosecutor threw at me to make me look like a horrible parent were statistics of many Indiana families, not just mine.

The Bible is very clear, we have all sinned and fall short of the glory of God (Romans 3:23). I made mistakes as a mother. Dakota made mistakes as a son. Despite those mistakes, I am *so* grateful from the bottom of my heart for redemption, for being saved from the price of bad decisions.

Without redemption, none of us could be saved from the choices we've made, big or small.

I find it ironic that redemption and restitution have the same meaning, one a religious term and the other legal. If a criminal must pay back a financial price for their crimes, why would one think there wouldn't be a price for smaller transgressions as well? An affair can cost you your marriage. Alcoholism can cost you your family. Lying on the job can cost you your career. Drinking a few glasses of wine at dinner can cost you your license. Having sex with the wrong person can cost you your sexual health or even your life.

All through the book of Jeremiah, God is very clear about the price of sin. Most of the time I read that book (which is often too deep for my comprehension), one common theme is that people have forgotten God and do what they want. We've forgotten to obey the two simplest commandments: trust and obey.

Religions sometimes make following God seem to be so hard, filled with rules and regulations. But really, if you just open the dusty covers of your Bible and read it for yourself, you'll find everything written in it is to teach you how to make good choices that lead to a long prosperous life. It truly has two rules, one asking you to trust God and the other to obey what He tells you to do. We get it all twisted up by adding all kinds of rituals and expectations to it.

Just like parents teaching their children, God teaches us. I taught Dakota to not do drugs because of what I saw it do in my own life. He chose to do drugs. He had to pay a price.

I taught Dakota to not steal. He chose to steal, therefore he had to pay a criminal price of time served in a maximum-security prison. God teaches us all throughout the Bible the way we should live. When we choose not to follow and go our own way, we therefore must pay the consequences. It's so easy to write this out on paper, but so hard to live out in real life.

Dakota's favorite verses are found in Romans. "Sin simply did what sin is so famous for doing: using the good as a cover to tempt me to do what would finally destroy me..." (Romans 7:13). "I know that all God's commands are spiritual, but I'm not. Isn't this also your experience? ...I've spent a lot of time in sin's prison. What I don't understand about myself is that I decide one way, but then I act another, doing things I absolutely despise. So, if I can't be trusted to figure out what is best for myself and then do it, it becomes obvious that God's command is necessary. But I need something more! For if I know the law but still can't keep it, and if the power of sin within me keeps sabotaging my best intentions, I obviously need help! I realize that I don't have what it takes. I can will it, but I can't do it; I decide to do good, but I don't really do it; I decide not to do bad, but then I do it anyway. My decisions, such as they are, don't result in actions. Something has gone wrong deep within me and gets the better of me every time" (Romans 7:14-23).

I knew that as a parent, my job was to discipline my child for doing wrong. I thought it was a phase he would grow out of. I should have picked more carefully the men I allowed to mentor my vulnerable son. Looking back, I should've perhaps locked him in my house and prevented him access to the outside world. I should've made him stay with me and violate parole, versus allowing him to go back to committing daytime burglaries. Dakota paid his price, and so have I, dearly.

Restoration

I've been trying to figure out how to live since that dreadful day I found out Dakota died. Even the simplest of things — doing my nails, cleaning house, making future plans — have felt, at times, impossible. I'm just struggling to get through the day. I have prayed numerous times for God to just show me what's next. I simply cannot wrap my head around the ending of our story. Let me remind you, suicide was *not* the way our story was supposed to end. He was not supposed to give up. He promised me they wouldn't bury him under the walls, yet he did.

I used to believe in the impossible. I used to be able to let my imagination run wild and dream big. Since Dakota's passing, it all now feels like a lie. How could I tell anyone to believe in the impossible, when our impossible situation ended so tragically, for the entire nation to see? How could I dream big and proclaim Luke 1:45 when I believed God would show up in a big way and dissolve a 68-turned-108-year sentence?

Why do bad things happen to good people? It's a universal question I've heard asked over and over through the years, including by me. Throughout my journey, I've never overlooked the consequences of my son's actions. No matter which side of this story you choose to be on, one must be able to relate that I didn't have a direct part to play regarding heroin use or the criminal actions. Regardless, I felt more heartache than I could ever have imagined. I've read before that drug addiction is a family sport; everyone gets to play.

Since Dakota's death, my entire life has turned upside down. Most days the energy it takes to exist is exhausting. Grief is a lifelong journey. There will never be a destination to reach where you will just "be over it."

To help me understand why bad things happen to good people, again I return to my friends in the Bible, specifically Moses. I've always struggled with Moses' story. He was one of the greatest leaders in the Old Testament. In Sunday school, we were always taught of his forty-year journey with the Israelites to get to the coveted Promised Land. We all remember that God gave Moses the Ten Commandments on stone tablets. Movies dramatize the parting of the Red Sea. Hearts melt when we read that God buried Moses himself in a hidden grave. What's always bothered me most is the question, "What did he do so bad that he wasn't allowed to enter the Promised Land?"

The answer to that question is found in the earlier chapters of Moses' life. He didn't live a life free of errors and mistakes. Remember his rap sheet included murder and evading arrest. He didn't trust God, which ultimately was the reason he wasn't able to enter the Promised Land (Numbers 20:12). Read that again — lack of trust! I can't begin to tell you how many times my trust crumbled. Just one mistake and he received the ultimate punishment, not able to taste the success of forty years of hard work. He even begged God to answer his prayer: "Let me cross over and see the good land" (Deuteronomy 3:25). God didn't. Moses died within view of his destination.

I have begged God also. "God, Dakota was just nineteen. It was one episode in time. I'm begging You to allow me to spend my later years with Dakota home. Please just give him forty years." You already know that prayer wasn't answered the way I wanted. But don't miss God's grace to all of Moses' mistakes. He is a God of justice, which is why Moses died; however, He is a God of mercy, as we can see in Deuteronomy 34:6 where God buried him Himself.

In my story, Dakota had to pay the price for his actions. Yet in the fullness of God's grace, He waited five long years for Dakota to surrender his heart and say, "Yes. I trust you, God, with my life." Dakota died before being able to live a full life, yet he was granted admission to the true Promised Land – Heaven.

Finally realizing all of this, I started to feel alive again. It was a gradual feeling; it wasn't like I just woke up one day and it all went away. It will never go away for me. I will miss Dakota every second of every minute for the rest of my life. However, now I can experience empathy, when once I could only experience sympathy. I view the world differently now.

I truly listen to the hurt in people's voices. When I tell someone I'll pray for them, I'm committed to sincerely pray and not just provide lip service.

I can honestly say I have no idea what the future holds for me. I've spent the last year and a half trying to cash in my membership to the "suicide of a child" and "my child is a drug addict turned prisoner" clubs. I despise every day of this, yet somehow love the compassion and depths of love I feel for others going through what I have, despite how small it may be compared to the tragedies of other stories.

I can finally dream of enjoying my other son, Derick. I'm so blessed to be able to be a mom to not just one but two sons. I always wanted another child so Dakota would never be alone, should something happen to me. Yet God knew twenty-two years ago how this story would play out. Derick wasn't for Dakota but for me. I never take for granted the decade Derick has given up for his brother's addiction. Derick forfeited his entire teenage years to be second to a brother who required Mom's full attention for medical or court issues. Derick never once complained. He always had the sweetest smile and made the most of his circumstance. All the things I felt like I lost when I buried Dakota, I will experience with Derick. I get to talk to Derick daily about his activities, from work to life skills. I'll get to watch Derick marry the love of his life. I'll get to dance at his wedding during the mother-son dance (which I've had to walk out of twice at other people's weddings since Dakota's passing, because it's just too much to watch). I'll get to be there for the day my first grandbaby is born. I'll get to attend birthday parties and many more life memories.

Despite having to bury a child, one must find enjoyment in the remainder of life. I know that for me, I have a profoundly greater love for the hurts of those around me. I can empathize with my patients entrusted in my nursing care. My heart melts when I have a mother share her story of her child's drug addiction. I know all too well the feeling of social shunning when your child commits the unthinkable. I know what it feels like to enter a courtroom and hear a guilty verdict time and time again.

All these lessons have taught me how to wrap my arms around women who are experiencing all I've experienced and let them know they're not alone. I love them, but most importantly Jesus loves them. There is life after addiction. There is life after incarceration. There is life after death. It's called redemption. Redemption is the key to set the prisoners free.

I don't think my loss compared to Dakota's victims' losses are the same. Their possessions can be replaced. No one ever had to bury a loved one because of Dakota. My loss is final. However, I do think of these people regularly in my life. I know what it feels like to have a thief in my house; a thief named heroin stole my son. I've prayed a thousand times for their forgiveness to Dakota. It won't change his circumstances, but it will release some of the pain they feel inside. I also pray for the return of their sense of security. I pray they may one day understand that he truly didn't target them specifically, nor intend to cause the heartache he did. He was driven to feed a demon.

Forgiveness is a sacred gift. Everyone throughout life is going to be on both ends of forgiveness. We all have moments where we will either need to give it or receive it. Forgiveness does not right the wrong. To me forgiveness simply means I humble myself to admit that I, too, make mistakes. I've been given the gift of mercy and compassion so many times in life, it's my duty to pay that forward to those who have hurt me.

In fall 2019, I was called into the lobby of my office. I had a visitor, a family member of a resident I had been in phone contact with but had never officially met. We'd already developed the sweetest friendship and had bonded over her family member. As I was walking down the hall and turned the corner, I saw a petite lady with dark curly hair and the most beautiful eyes standing at the desk. I walked up thinking, *I know her from somewhere.* I quickly reached out my hand, and we officially met and introduced ourselves. I kept asking, "Where do I know you from?"

She let go of my hand, hugged me, and whispered in my ear, "I'm sorry about your son." Suddenly it all came flooding back. A year prior I sat in a courtroom and listened to this polished woman on the stand rehashing all she went through, coming home to finding her house burglarized by Dakota. She was so angry and bitter. Honestly, after listening to the same victim statement over and over, TV after TV, gold jewelry after gold jewelry, so was I. My son was already serving a heinous amount of time and they just kept piling it up. I was angry and wasn't as sympathetic as I'd been at the beginning. We both left that courtroom that day and went our separate ways. We were divided over our emotions for a young man, my son. She wanted him to pay, and I wanted him to be shown mercy. Her testimony sealed another twenty-year sentence added to what he was already serving.

As fate would have it, a year later we found ourselves in the same situation, standing in a room staring at each other. This time, we both shared compassion in our heart for a mutual man, this time her family member. Unknown to either of us all those times on the phone was that I was the mother of the young man who had wrecked her life. I was building a friendship with the woman who wanted to send my son to prison for an additional twenty years, on top of sixty-eight.

I will never, *ever*, forget her hug. It was showered in forgiveness, compassion, and mercy. She kept saying she was sorry. I kept saying I was sorry. We were both sorry for the pain the other was feeling. That was the one of most unforgettable moments of this story, and one I'll treasure forever.

She allowed me the opportunity to share with her who Dakota really was, before heroin. I shared with her pictures of a beautiful young boy who didn't compare to the young man she saw in a prison-issued jumpsuit with chains around his waist, hands, and feet She listened intently as I tried to explain the madness behind what had happened to her. I wanted her to know that she was not targeted out by a vicious, evil person, and that I just wanted her to feel safe again.

Since that day, we've stayed in close contact, and she'll remain a pillar of forgiveness in my life. She needed to have closure with my son and I needed to forgive her.

According to the Christian Apologetics & Research Ministry, the word 'forgive' is found 119 times in the King James Version of the Bible. As I was writing this book, several words kept circling back to me: forgiveness, compassion, redemption, and restoration. Each is defined by Google in the following ways:

Forgive: To stop feeling resentment or anger against someone. To cancel a debt

Compassion: Sympathetic concern of others' distresses, together with a desire to alleviate it

Redemption: Being saved from sin. Gaining something in exchange for something

Restoration/Restitution: Bringing back or giving an equivalent for an injury

If you talk to anyone who has struggled with drug addiction, you will hear these words shared among every story — pain, depression, low self-esteem, guilt over the hurt they've caused, shame over the things they've done. Shame is the key that locks the prison door, but mercy is the key to unlock it.

I think the one thing through this entire experience that's bothered me the most is the lack of compassion society has for those with these struggles, including myself at one time. By the grace of God, I've never known the power a pill can hold over someone. I've never known what it feels like to sell your soul for a line of powdery substances. I couldn't imagine having it all and walking away to chase a high that is hellbent on destroying me.

I've learned through writing this book, and from rereading my Bible cover to cover, that no one is perfect. Everyone commits sins, every single day. We each need forgiveness. We all create false idols in our lives to replace the one true God who should be in our lives. We all want forgiveness for our wrongs. We all want compassion when we're hurting. We all desire redemption and to repay our wrongs. We all want restitution for the things taken from us.

My prayer is for you to do some serious soul searching. When society doesn't want to deal with an issue, we choose to lock away the problem so we never have to look at it again. I pray this story will open the eyes and hearts of all who may read this. I pray we will start treating addiction as the individual problem it is. I pray we will understand that crime is inherently associated with addiction. I pray for judicial reform and justice. I would've totally understood a verdict of ten years for those stolen items, but not a life sentence. I pray we will start placing more emphasis on dealing with our children and the issues they're facing in a world that is racing around them. I beg that we go back to the fundamentals of the importance of family. I hope we will teach everyone within our three-feet space of the loving, compassionate, and forgiving spirit of the God we serve.

I truly don't know how the end of our particular story will look. I refuse to accept suicide as the last words in Dakota's final chapter. I can only hope that sharing this will help even just one family, and save one young man from making the same choices and suffering the same consequences as Dakota. For that, I will be able to find some relief in my broken heart.

I encourage anyone reading this book to ask yourself, "What can I do with my story? How can I honor God with my life?" Your words may be the key to unlocking someone else's prison.

Dear Dakota

If you are in a prison reading this book, this is my prayer for you as your surrogate momma, just as I would write my last letter to my son…

Hi _____ (fill in your name),
You were on my mind, so I thought I'd take a few minutes and drop you a short note. I know I don't get to write as often as I'd like, but please don't think you aren't in my mind, spirit and heart every second of the day.
It's November! Wow, where has the year gone already? As the nights are turning chillier, I worry about you having enough blankets. Are you staying warm? Can you believe in just a few weeks you will be twenty-six?!
So, what's new in your world? Any new slam recipes? Any new friends? How is your program going? Your brother is doing great. He misses you, even if he doesn't write. He's just young and trying to figure out his way.
So much has happened, and time just seems to keep moving on. I know your greatest fear is being forgotten. I know your friends have seemed to fall away, but I promised you I never

would, and I will keep that promise until I inhale my last breath.

I've had a few years to reflect on what got us to this spot. These weren't the hopes and dreams I had for you; neither was this the life I imagined for you. When I close my eyes and allow my mind to go to where you are, all I can feel is cold and darkness. It's impossible for me to ask "How are you feeling?" because I can only imagine. Honestly, I just don't have the strength to bear that heartache. I hear the loss of hope in your voice and see the look of depression in your eyes.

*There is absolutely **nothing** I can possibly do to take this from you. I've drained my bank accounts and hired every attorney I could find to take your case. This is it. This is as far as our human capabilities can perform. It is now 100 percent surrender. I must surrender you over to the care of Jesus. He promised me years ago He would protect you. When we reach our end is where God begins.*

*Now, **you** must submit your heart to God. The first step is admitting to Him every shameful thing you've ever done. Even those things tucked away in your soul that you've never whispered to anyone. You must be willing to admit that this is way too big for you. You need Him. I cannot do this part for you. You must open the door of your heart to Him.*

I pray you have ears to hear Jesus. I pray that you will drop to your precious knees tonight and beg God to forgive you of your sins. Accountability is the first requirement.

It's time to surrender. You must surrender your pride. As much I love you, all the parts of you, God loves you more despite your darkest sins.

At this point, all He is asking of you is to trust and obey. Trust what He is laying on your heart to be true. Obedience requires an act of blind faith on your part, despite what those around you may think. Be the warrior you were created to be.

No matter the time limit you must serve, you still have purpose. Please look around you. Look for those who are younger than you and desire to have a role model in their life. Their momma is depending on you to show them the ropes of prison etiquette, just like those men before you showed you.

I can't fathom why the culture in prison must be one of such distrust and hate. The common theme behind those bars is that everyone screwed up and everyone got caught. Everyone is far away from their families. Everyone has lost it all! Everyone needs to start showing each other what they desire from society — forgiveness, kindness, and to not be forgotten.

I love you with all my heart and always will,
Mom

Final Words

Dear Friends,

Through this writing, I pray you don't misinterpret my heart. I'm not trying to right Dakota's wrongs or soften the hurt in his victims. My entire goal of writing this story was to magnify the stunning glory of God's undeserving grace.

I've spent years replaying everything wrong about our story, which I'm prepared for many to do after reading this. Yet all I can do is surrender my heart to the feet of Jesus. I can't take my eyes off an innocent man at the cross hanging next to a thief like my son. I can't stop feeling what His mother must have felt glancing over my way, her son innocent to save mine who wasn't.

I'm in awe of the majesty of God's mercy. I will for the rest of my life tell the story of His love and forgiveness. I will strive to be as forgiving as the lady on our stand. I will try my hardest to be as loyal as Dakota was. I will never forget the importance of family. I will be a better mother to Derick.

I will provide compassionate nursing care to those entrusted in me. I will be compassionate to those I see on the side of the road holding a homeless sign. I will drop to my knees and thank God with the utmost sincerity for His forgiveness of my sins, no matter how little they are.

I pray you too will do all the above and so much more. Always remember, God has a special place in His heart for widows, orphans, and prisoners, therefore so should we.

In the final words of my precious son, my prayer for you is that you too will live your best life, despite what others think. Remember, you only have one life to live and you need to live it to the fullest! Thank you for reading my story! May you always believe in the impossible and dream big!

Vanessa

References

Addictions. The Crisis in Indiana. Indiana University. Accessed October 5, 2020. https://addictions.iu.edu/understanding-crisis/crisis-in-indiana.html.

Christian Apologetics & Research Ministry. How many times do various words appear in the Bible? https://carm.org/how-many-times-do-various-words-appear-in-the-bible . Accessed November 6, 2020.

Keller, Josh and Pearce, Adam. "A Small Indiana County Sends More People to Prison Than San Francisco and Durham, N.C., Combined. Why?" *The New York Times*, September 2, 2016. https://www.nytimes.com/2016/09/02/upshot/new-geography-of-prisons.html. Accessed January 8, 2020.

Key Substance Use and Mental Health Indicators in the United States: Results from the 2018 National Survey on Drug Use and Health. May, 2019. Accessed October 5, 2020. https://store.samhsa.gov/product/key-substance-use-and-mental-health-indicators-in-the-united-states-results-from-the-2018-national-survey-on-Drug-Use-and-Health/PEP19-5068.

Opioid Epidemic. Indiana State Department of Health. Accessed October 5, 2020. https://www.in.gov/mph/930.htm.

Lavender, George. "Private Contractor Accused of Skimping on Prisoner Food". January 30, 2014. Accessed March 28, 2021. https://inthesetimes.com/article/private-contractor-accused-of-skimping-on-prisoner-food.

The Annie E. Casey Foundation. Kids Count Data Center. Accessed October 5, 2020. https://datacenter.kidscount.org/data#USA/2/23/2488,24,2592,26,2721/char/0.

Made in the USA
Columbia, SC
23 October 2023